CROWOOD COLLECTORS' SERIES

Golf Memorabilia

KEVIN McGIMPSEY

THE CROWOOD PRESS

First published in 2008 by
The Crowood Press Ltd
Ramsbury, Marlborough
Wiltshire SN8 2HR

www.crowood.com

British Library Cataloguing-in-Publication Data
A catalogue record for this book is available from the British Library.

ISBN 978 1 84797 063 3

Typeset by Simon Loxley
Printed and bound in Singapore by Craft Print International

ACKNOWLEDGEMENTS

This book is dedicated to my long-time golfing partner and friend, David J. Daniels, who died too young, on the golf course, in March 2008.

My sincere thanks are extended to the following people who made my life much easier than it could have been while researching and writing this book: to Bob Dukeson, Bonhams (get well soon) for editing an early draft; Bob Gowland, Bob Gowland International Golf Auctions, for the use of several important golfing images; Brad Cuvelier, Williamson, New York, golf ball collector, for allowing me to use images of his golf ball collection; Brian Cole, Bonhams' director, for his input and guidance on all ten chapters; David Easby, established collector, for his input and guidance on many aspects; David Neech, Sotheby's 1983 to 2000, for encouraging me to write golf books, and for his general help, expertise and friendship; Tony Harrolds for his expertise on cards of all shapes and sizes.

Also to David K.C. Wright, Director of Regions and Heritage, The P.G.A., for his help with the Ryder Cup section; Don Jaime Ortiz-Patino, past President, Club de Golf, Valderrama, Spain, for the use of several important photographs; Dr Gary Wiren, North Palm Beach, Florida, for allowing me to use photographs of his extensive collection; Nick Sample for his great artwork; George Petro, New York, medal collector, for his initial help with the medal section; Graham Budd, Graham Budd Auctions, for the use of several significant golfing images; Howard J. Schickler, Sarasota, Florida, for his expertise and help with the photograph section; Jim Espinola, Pelham, New Hampshire, antique golf collector and long-time friend, for allowing me to use images of his wonderful collection; John Hanna, Captain of the British Golf Collectors Society 2006–2008, for sharing his knowledge of golfing ephemera; Norman Fox, established book collector, for his knowledge, penmanship and enthusiasm; Peter Helweg, Richmond, Virginia, established ceramics and glass specialist, for his input and for allowing me to use images of his beautiful golfing ceramics and glassware collection.

Also to Rachel Doerr, Lyon and Turnbull director, for the use of their many important golfing images; Roger Morton, at Golfer Today, good friend and auction house golf specialist, for his unstinting help with the golf clubs' chapter; Sarah Fabian-Baddiell, at Golfiana, for the photograph of what is probably the only surviving Silver Queen figurine; Stephen Grimoldby, for his help with the Open programmes section; Thomas J. Lommen, senior specialist at P.B.A. Galleries, San Francisco, for the use of several significant golfing images and his input to the book section; David Kirkwood of Alex Kirkwood & Son, for his insight into golfing trophies and medals; and finally to my fellow Bonhams' colleagues, who have all helped me in their own ways, including Antony Bennett, Alexander Clement, Jane Elston, Caroline Morrell, Andrew Spicer, Jonathon O'Marah, Mark French and Laura Baynes.

INTRODUCTION

In comparison to more traditional ones such as art, ceramics, and jewellery, the golf memorabilia market is very young and immature. It is certainly not a market to enter to make a quick profit. If that is your aim, then please try somewhere else.

Harry B. Wood was the first documented collector of golf memorabilia. During the 1880s and early 1900s, he sought golfing relics north of the border, using a small but active team of lookers and scouts who would source material for him. He even befriended Old Tom Morris who sold him clubs and balls. In 1910 Wood published the first dedicated book on golf antiques, *Golfing Curios and the Like*. During the first half of the twentieth century there were only a handful of books that covered memorabilia, old equipment, bygone implements etc. These focused on the historical perspective of the game rather than being aimed solely at collectors.

In the late 1970s and early 1980s, the three major auction houses, Sotheby's, Christies and Phillips (now Bonhams), identified a potential market in golf and all three had sales comprising a variety of long-nose clubs, feather and gutta-percha golf balls and early artwork. With each year, the market became more and more established. Auctions also took place in the USA and two independent Golf Collectors Societies were formed, one in America in the early 1980s and the other in Britain a few years later. Both are still thriving.

The young golf market was dramatically upset in 1990. At this time the Japanese economy was so buoyant that company directors with a plentiful business assets and a passion for golf embarked on decorating their offices with golfing artefacts; this was also legitimate tax avoidance. At the July 1990 sales in the UK, a couple of Japanese buyers wreaked havoc by buying between them some fifty-five per cent of the 1,500 lots on offer. Many established dealers and collectors found it hard to outbid them on the good items. When they did, they found themselves paying up to three times what they had thought they would pay.

At the back of many minds was the thought that maybe this was the way it would be from then on. Collectors reeled in disbelief at the prices being achieved; some in the short term who sold made a lot of money, while some tried to match the Japanese, believing that this was now the norm and that prices would never be at pre-1988 levels. One summer they were there, literally buying everything, and the next year they were gone. Why? Because the world was in a huge recession and money was very, very tight.

Prices came back to earth with a bump and many fell even below the level that had been achieved in the middle 1980s. However bloodied and bruised, the golf memorabilia market has over the last fifteen years or so got itself back to a point where prices and values at auction are just about fair to both buyers and sellers. In other words, although the market is still a little fragile, it is both a good enough time to buy and a good time to sell.

The golf memorabilia market is a microcosm of the antique market in general, where it is virtually impossible to sell inferior or damaged items unless they are exceptionally rare. Quality remains a paramount consideration, whether it be mint condition golf balls in their wrappers; first edition books still with their dust jackets; lightly coloured wooden clubs in preference to those in dark wood; or ceramics free of cracks and paintings that are signed and preferably dated.

Although the fun of collecting is most definitely in the search, it is just as important to be knowledgeable. I hope that this book imparts to the reader at least some new piece of information that may help in the decision process to make a purchase or to sell an item.

Happy collecting!

Kevin W. McGimpsey
July 2008

From feather balls to wrapped balls, these balls cover
100 years of the game.

GOLF BALLS, COUNTER DISPLAYS AND GOLF TEES

The Golf Ball

The following is a true anecdote by David Neech, Sotheby's golf consultant 1981–2000:

> Golf clubs throughout the country often have their rare items on display behind glass, but don't know what they own. I visited a club in Sussex in 1985 that had a fives ball (an ancient game similar to squash) in a display case labelled 'A 19th Century Feathery' that had been donated by a member. When I hesitantly pointed out the error I was berated by the secretary for not knowing my subject, but it transpired that the offending ball had for years sat unprotected on the clubhouse mantelpiece, and a switch had obviously taken place.

Ouch!

Why start this book with the golf ball? Simply because to play a game of golf the three single most important constituents are the ball, the club and the course. The ball in its four major stages of evolution has led the development of the club and the golf course…so we will start with the earliest recognized golf ball, the feather ball.

THE FEATHER GOLF BALL

Feather golf balls range in price from £1,000 upwards to £40,000. They were made in Scotland from the sixteenth century up until late into the nineteenth century, the 1870s. Many of the ball makers have been well documented over the years, such as Douglas Gourlay of Brunstfield (also spelt Burntsfield), who was a ball maker in the 1780s. His two sons John and William continued the business in the 1800s. Another is David Marshall, who made his feather balls in and around 1830; he is a much sought-after ball maker. Tom Morris was a great golfer, club maker and skilled feather ball maker; any surviving feather golf balls stamped with his name sell at a premium of at least twice the norm. The Robertson family made great golf balls too, and balls by William Robertson *circa* the 1790s, and his famous nephew 'Allan' Robertson, are much sought after.

Making a feather ball is a bit like key-hole surgery.

Allan Robertson was one of the top nineteenth-century ball makers.

The number 27 denoted the weight of the ball in dwt: approximately 1.48oz.

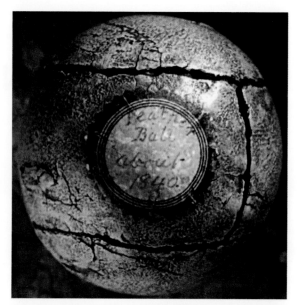

A J. Gourlay ball inscribed in pen: 'Presented to me by Mr Alexander at St Andrews September 95. In his possession for over 40 years, one of the old leather balls played with by him in the early fifties.'

This ball retains the sticker of one of the first collectors, Harry B. Wood.

The majority of feather balls comprised three pieces of leather. The ball maker cut out these pieces from a section of boiled and untanned bull's hide, two round ones for the poles, and one a strip to make the middle area of the ball. After shaping the pieces and softening them, small holes were punched in the end flaps of the middle piece to make it easier to stitch them together with waxed linen thread. A small hole was left, through which the feathers would be stuffed, but first the small leather sack was turned outside in through this small hole. This was a very difficult procedure, and not everyone could master it, and the thicker the leather (to make a heavy ball), the harder it was to perform this task. With the stitches inside the ball, these potentially

COLLECTORS' HELPFUL HINTS

- Does the ball still have its maker's name? If it does, this is good, because a named ball is worth at least twice that of an unnamed ball. If it has a name or number, hold the ball in your hand at arm's length and see if you can read the name on the ball: if yes, then it is a good clear stamp; if not, then that will be a negative factor when it comes to commercial worth.

- What of its condition? Usually mint feather balls are the ones that were not played with. They may have been a prize to be treasured, or they may in time, as often appears to be the case, end up in an old desk's drawer for decades, if not centuries. Nevertheless, feather golf balls showing their age with split seams will still have a monetary value (£1,000 plus).

- As regards storage, golf balls don't do well under bright lights and in warm conditions, so display feather golf balls as you would all other golf balls, and try to keep them dry and cool.

BUYER BEWARE

LATERAL HAZARDS

✳ A feather golf ball can be rock hard, while others have just the slightest give when the leather is pressed down. Beware: there are fakes, and these vary from very good to very poor. Look out for the wrong coloured twine keeping the ball together; look out for leather, similar to dirtied chamois, that has been aged and used to cover a hard, round object such as a modern golf ball. This modern material has been glued to stay in place, and some may even have the name of the supposed ball maker, such as Allan.

A fine J. Gourlay feather ball on the left with its concealed stitching, and a fives ball on the right showing its stitches.

✳ Don't mistake a fives ball for a feathery. The fives ball looks like a combination of a feathery and a baseball; it is constructed from five leather petals, with its stitches on the outside rather than the inside, and is worth at best only £5.

RIGHT: *The ball on the left purports to be an Allan Robertson feather, but it is a fake. The other ball is a reproduction feather and is made from resin.*

weak spots were afforded a small degree of protection from the golf club.

In the meantime, the goose down, or 'cocks and hens' chicken feathers, were boiled in a mixture of alum and water to soften them up. Tradition has it that the amount of feathers needed to make one feather ball was the same as the amount that filled a top hat. In fact a ball needed more feathers than this. The flaccid sack of leather was put into a supportive device, such as a cup-shaped stand or a leather collar; the latter had an opening to enable the ball maker to get at the leather casing. The soggy feathers were then forcibly stuffed through the small slit with small, sharply pointed tools. When the sack was nearly full, the ball maker placed a long metal awl called a brogue under his arm: this

crutch-like implement enabled him to force even more feathers into the sack. He used callipers to determine the diameter and size of the ball, and scales to ensure that the ball was the correct weight. The finished ball was seldom round, but more egg-shaped, and as such was well suited to the rough and uneven texture of the putting surface.

The slit was sewn up with a simple stitch, and this was the only one visible. The ball maker then applied a liberal coat of pure, well ground white lead paint; when this had dried, another coat was applied. Later, iron callipers with wooden handles were made to hold the ball in position. The ball maker's name and the weight were often hand-written or stamped on to the ball in dark blue or black ink. Feather golf balls were weighted and

The Holy Grail for golf ball collectors: a Paterson Composite ball.

Note the raised rim at the ball's equator – a 'must have' characteristic to be a genuine, smooth gutta-percha ball.

sized to suit the maker's clientèle, and this was usually stamped on to the ball as a two-digit number in the high twenties.

Often to demonstrate a club and/or ball apprentice's skills, the principal would task his students to go small, just as was the case for furniture pupils. Clubs would be replicated in 1/16 scale to be perfect examples of real-sized clubs, and the same was done with golf balls. One such feather ball came to auction in the late 1990s. A dealer circulated the story at the saleroom that this ball had come from the Queen Anne dolls' house kept at Windsor Castle, and that it wasn't a real feather golf ball at all. However, it was a roguish attempt to turn other potential bidders off the ball, and in fact the miniature feather ball had originally belonged to a golf club in the Adelaide area of Australia. The Robertson family of club and ball makers had emigrated to Australia in the 1850s, and because David Roberston, Allan's father, had in all probability made it, it sold for £8,200.

What does the two-digit number denote that is often found on the golf ball? Golf historians are still unsure which system the early ball makers used to denote the weight of the golf ball. But a popular system for recording the weight of gold was the troy system, in

which one pennyweight (dwt) weighed 24g, and it is likely that this was the system used in Scotland by the ball makers. The equivalent of a feather ball weighing, for example, 30dwt was 1.65oz!

The peak of feather ball making was in the late 1840s, and this reflected the upsurge in the game's popularity. But 1850 spelled big trouble for the feather ball, its supporters and makers, because there was soon to be a new kid on the block: the Paterson's Composite all solid gutta-percha golf ball.

PATERSON'S COMPOSITE, THE FIRST SOLID RUBBER BALL

The chances of finding a Paterson's Composite ball are remote because there are fewer than four known to exist. It isn't even certain who Paterson was.

The most believable story is that in 1850 a Reverend Paterson in St Andrews made a prototype golf ball from gutta-percha materials recently arrived at his father's house from the Far East. Why he decided to do so remains a mystery, but according to folklore he rolled the rubber into a ball and took it on to the nearby links and played some shots. There were many teething problems that included the ball breaking up, but his

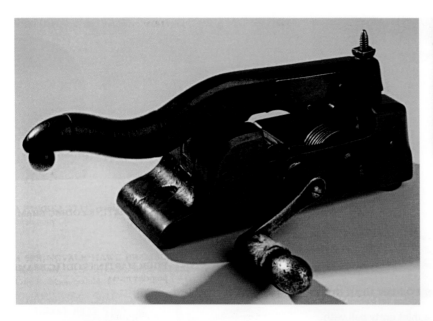

LEFT: This ball marker dates to 1860 and was used by Willie Dunn Senior.
ABOVE: An early and rare example of a gutty ball with vertical cuts in the style of Dunn.

A fine example of an unnamed gutty ball made from a mould.

'saintly' perseverance won through and within a short period the ball was good enough to be marketed as the 'Paterson's Composite'.

Those that have been seen are painted in a light green-brown colour closely resembling the feather ball; it was a similar size but was rounder. The ball makers in St Andrews soon realized the commercial worth of this new product, though some were more astute than others. Allan Robertson regarded them as being bad for the game and for his feather ball-making business, while his understudy Tom Morris was quick to see that this was part of the game's future. He and others, and eventually Robertson too, made their own versions of the new, smooth-patterned rubber golf ball. Within a short period the players realized that these balls when marked by their hacking whilst playing, had better aerodynamics than when in perfect smooth condition.

COLLECTORS' HELPFUL HINTS

- Is your ball a gutta-percha golf ball, or a later, rubber-cored ball? Try the 'clink-clink' test: gently tap the ball with a hammer, or knock it on a hard surface, and if it sounds like a piece of ceramic china, the odds are that it is a gutty ball.

- It can be difficult to distinguish between what is purported to be a smooth gutty, and what is just a rubber core from a post-1902 golf ball. A clue to its being the genuine object is size, in that it should be big, with an impressive diameter of over 1.6in (4cm) and still with its tell-tale fin or rim around its diameter, caused by the joining of the two hemispherical moulds. These smooth, covered balls were only made for a maximum of a couple of years, so are rare and expensive. Best to err on the side of caution, because the experts are of the opinion that for every twenty possibles, only one is the real thing.

What every ball collector wants: a mint gutty ball with the brass mould that made it.

Beware of fakes and imitations. An Eclipse golf ball advertisement in the 1880s.

The solid gutta-percha golf ball had superseded the feather ball by the end of the nineteenth century. The great ball makers, such as Robertson, Morris, Dunn and Forgan, all added their own distinctive hand-hammered patterns to their golf balls – and it was no easy feat chiselling away with the end of a claw hammer a pattern to make the ball not only aerodynamic but also aesthetically pleasing.

From the 1870s, ingenious machines resembling a wood-maker's plane, which etched criss-crossed lines into the ball, replaced the hammer. By the 1880s, golf ball moulds not only made the ball, but also its cover pattern. The mesh-lined pattern was popular until the arrival of the brambled pattern of pimples in the 1880s; this new cover pattern soon became the big favourite with golfers.

The late 1890s was a time of imitation, invention, patents and the creation of cover designs that some have called 'works of art'.

Genuine smooth gutta-percha golf balls were only made for five to ten years, and are undervalued in comparison with featheries that were made for centuries.

An interesting aside to the golf ball market are the numbers, albeit small, that are being discovered on old courses during course excavations, especially in areas of

Currie's Eclipse golf ball, *circa* 1870.

sand dunes that were originally in play. Sand (unlike water) looks after its deposited treasures – for that is what they are. In 1999 the green-keeping staff at the New Luffness Golf Club found a near-mint Tom Morris hand-hammered gutty that sold at auction for £9,000.

LEFT: Willie Dunn's very patriotic Stars and Stripes ball, circa 1897.
BELOW: Balfour gutta-percha golf balls: the finest Scottish-made, *circa* 1886.

CENTRE: Red paint helped the ball to stand out on frost- or daisy-covered fairways.
BOTTOM: Superb condition and clean markings – a great ball from the 1880s.

The Chambers patented machine was used to print names on the golf ball.

"HOME" PATENT GOLF BALL PRESS.

Golf says: "Judging from our experiments and the nicely marked ball which was promptly turned out, we should say that it will be found eminently satisfactory, not only for remaking balls but for making new ones." "The pressure that can be applied by hand is really enormous."

The Field says: "We have subjected the Press to a thorough trial, and have every confidence in recommending it." "We remoulded a beautifully marked ball." "Full of life and elasticity."

In two sizes, No. 1 producing a "27" Ball, and No. 2 a "27½." To be obtained of all dealers in Golfing Material and of the Company, price **10s** post free, **10s. 6d.** For Repainting, we recommend our "Elastic" Paint, warranted not to chip or crack. Price **1s. 6d.** per tin, post free, **1s. 9d.**

"HOME" GOLF BALL PRESS COMPANY,
24, HOWARD STREET, GLASGOW.

LEFT: This ball press was advertised in 1892.
ABOVE: A hand-held press enabled golfers to recycle their damaged gutty golf balls.

THE 'MODERN' RUBBER-CORED GOLF BALL

The year 1898 heralded the arrival, or invention of, basically what is today's golf ball, the first golf ball with a core, around which was wound rubber thread; this was then covered in gutta-percha and patterned.

Coburn Haskell, the inventor, was a retired businessman, and he contacted a friend, Bertram G. Work, who worked at, and later became President of B. F. Goodrich Tire and Rubber Company. Haskell had come up with the idea of a compressed rubber ball made from cut-up rubber strips that were stretched and wound into a ball. Haskell made a prototype, and Work produced a gutta-percha moulded cover to encapsulate Haskell's rubber-cored ball. In April 1899 the two men patented their three-piece wound ball. Production at Goodrich was greatly increased by state of the art, purpose-built machines that could wind the rubber at great speeds and maintain a degree of uniformity, too.

The original (Type 1) Haskell ball had a cover compris-

BUYER BEWARE

TIGHT LIES

✳ Beware of what are purported to be smooth golf ball moulds that would have made smooth-patterned gutta-percha golf balls in the 1850s! Yes, they are indeed smooth, but only because they were not engraved with a cover pattern; in other words, they dated to the 1880s rather than the 1850s.

✳ There are known reproductions, and these are sometimes passed off as the real thing. A good example is the glassed box of Silvertown balls, produced as samples in the 1920s. They are all real balls, some of which were produced from genuine moulds at the time to make up the required quantities. One of the balls is smooth and is stamped in capitals, 'SILVERTOWN'. When the lettering has faded or been wiped, this reproduction has been passed off as a real 1850s smooth gutta-percha ball.

A fine selection of gutty and rubber-cored balls.

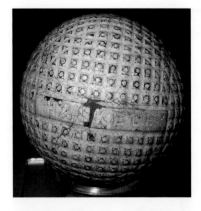

It is thought that there are fewer than twenty surviving examples of the Haskell Type 1 ball.

This 'Remade' Haskell Type 1 ball is even rarer than the Haskell ball, and only one has been recorded.

ing small sunken squares, each with a tiny pin-sized dot within. This ball is extremely rare: not only have few survived, probably fewer than ten, but those that have are invariably in poor condition, with badly cracked covers.

In 1900 James Foulis, the professional at the Chicago Golf Club, had played with a ball that he had remould-ed in his workshop – and he had not noticed that it was one of those new-fangled Haskell balls! He had used a mould that had given the ball the popular bramble pattern (Type 2) cover instead of the mesh and dot pattern. Whilst playing with it he was most impressed with the ball's distance and accuracy; he cut it open to investigate, and was amazed to discover that it had a core of rubber threads.

Foulis later reported his findings to B. F. Goodrich, namely how good a ball was the Haskell with a bramble cover pattern. In 1902 Sandy Herd used his one and only Type 2 Haskell golf ball to win the 1902 Open Championship at Royal Liverpool. In the same year Laurence (Lawrie) Auchterlonie played with similar Haskell golf balls to win the US Open.

The Type 1 Haskell ball was only produced between 1899 and 1900. Demand for them remains very high, no matter what their condition.

Such a box of mint Haskell brambles would fetch at least £5,000 at auction.

ABOVE: A superb Army & Navy CSL No. 1 ball with paper bag, *circa* very early 1900s.
LEFT: Originally the Henry's Rifle, it was changed to the name of the manufacturer, Henley.

ABOVE: This Army & Navy CSL No. 2 ball with paper bag was found in an attic in Germany in 2006.

The 'Map of the World' ball, made by J. P. Cochrane in 1908. There are fewer than twenty surviving examples.

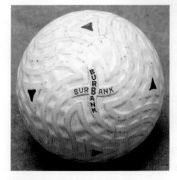

Stow Woodward introduced their Burbank ball with wavy swirls in the early 1930s.

This Finnigan's Corona patent 'Indestructible Ball' is only one of two known, and sold at auction in 2006 for just under £4,000.

ABOVE: An unusual cover pattern, and great to have the ball and its mould.

LEFT: Even as late as the 1930s the ball makers were still producing 'works of art'.

The North British 'Chick' ball, *circa* early 1910s, with a pattern of interlinked dots.

Golf ball production, for obvious reasons, declined to nothing during the Great War years.

MORE COVER PATTERNS

The major twentieth-century ball landmark was the registration of the round dimple design in 1905. To emphasize its significance, today most golf balls have cover patterns made up of dimples.

Spalding bought the rights to the dimple design, and for several years the other ball manufacturers could not call their pattern 'dimple' and had to come up with other shapes and patterns. This was a great time for invention and imagination. Sometimes the cover patterns were made to stand out and probably were not tested for their aerodynamic qualities. Dimples were renamed as discs, hollows, indentations, recesses.

In 1933 the American firm, the Faroid Company, launched the Faroid golf ball, which was unusual for two reasons. First, its cover was made of a very thin celluloid material and so there was no need to apply the

ABOVE: Such golf ball shop dispenser tins are extremely rare, as few have survived. The brass mould was used to make the Excelsior bramble ball.

LEFT: This Minikahada ball was auctioned in 2006 and fetched a record price for a bramble when it sold for $10,516.

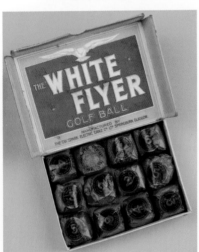

ABOVE: ` This box of Ace balls is enhanced with its 1929 flyer.

LEFT: What a shame that one ball label is missing! Even so, a great box of balls, circa 1930.

ABOVE: A J. P. Cochrane bramble circa 1904, still retaining its original wax paper wrapper.

LEFT: A beautiful Silver King S bramble ball, circa 1910.

ABOVE: St Mungo
Manufacturing introduced
the Colonel Blue Ring ball
in 1924. The parachute ball
was an early practice
device.

LEFT: Boxed sets from the
1950s, all the balls still with
their original wrappers.

normal coats of paint. Second, those raised concentric ridges that run around the ball were designed to reduce the ball's flight hooking or slicing! The ball was stamped 'This End Up' so the player positioned the it on the tee correctly. The '75' reflected its selling price of 75 cents.

Golf ball collectors regard the 1970s as being the cut-off date for balls that are collectible. Why? Because this was when the small 1.62in (4cm) ball began to be phased out by the R & A.

SIGNATURE GOLF BALLS

This pastime consists of collecting golf balls with the name or signature of a player, and it spans an era from the Patterson Composite up to the present day.

Harry Vardon is known even by beginners of the

RIGHT: These
Sparkbrook
Kestrel golf
balls were
made in the
1930s.

ABOVE: The original
signature ball...the Vardon
Flyer gutty ball.
LEFT: Ball collectors enthuse
over 'Hole in One' letters from
the ball manufacturers.

COLLECTORS' HELPFUL HINTS

- Golf balls are easy to display, they don't take up
  space, and there are many collecting themes,
  such as collecting only mesh-patterned balls, or
  just wrapped balls, or just small sized balls
  (1.62in), or signature balls, or logo balls.

- Negative factors that affect value include loss
  of paint or strike marks.

- Hairline cracks usually caused by heat will
  turn into big cracks; in time the ball may even
  explode.

- Try not to buy balls that have been recovered
  from water hazards; these are known as 'lake'
  balls. Over the years – in some cases in excess of
  one hundred – the water can seep into the ball,
  or the lack of pressure on the ball
  causes it to become unstable.

game because of the renowned Vardon grip that he
made famous by using, rather than inventing. One of
the earliest signature golf balls is the Vardon Flyer (spelt
Flier in America). Spalding paid Vardon to play with
their equipment, and in 1899 they launched their new
gutty bramble-patterned golf ball, the Vardon Flyer.
Spalding persuaded Vardon to tour the USA to play literally hundreds of exhibitions and golf matches against
local professionals, and to promote 'his' ball – and this
he did with some success. But then from nowhere came
the news that one of Spalding's main competitors, the
Goodrich Tyre Co., had pioneered a new type of golf
ball (the rubber-cored Haskell ball) that would make
all the gutty balls obsolete. The American tour was
therefore brought to an abrupt end – though before
returning home, Vardon won the 1900 US Open at the
Chicago Golf Club with a Vardon Flyer golf ball.

LOGO GOLF BALLS

Logos on golf balls have been used for many years
by golf clubs and businesses as mini-billboards advertising their brands or course. In 2007, over 25 per cent of
the 600 million golf balls produced annually were logo
golf balls.

GOLF BALL ADVERTISING FIGURINES

During the 1930s, 1940s and 1950s, British ball manufacturers supplied club professionals, who sold their product with countertop advertising figurines. These were provided free for display on the shop counter, with the aim of encouraging sales. The Golf Ball Development Company in its advertisements featured a cheeky-looking but smartly attired golfer wearing plus fours and a large baggy hat. His cheeks were puffed, and he smoked either a small black pipe or a fake cigarette. He was presented on a wooden plinth that carried one of two slogans , either 'He Played a Penfold' or 'He Played a Bromford', advertising their two bestselling golf balls. Accordingly he was known as either the Penfold Man or the Bromford Man. The figures, made from papier-mâché that had been moulded and then painted, were produced between 1930 and 1939, and for a few years after the war, by Harris & Sheldon Company, located close to Golf Ball Development in Birmingham.

Several moulds must have been used over the years because minor variations occur. The height of the figure varies around 20in (50cm), and there are different styles of plinth. Figures that were made in the 1930s have a gap between the legs from the shoes up to the plus fours, and the face and shoes are sharper and more detailed than in later figures.

There are two plinth types. Early types measure 2⁷⁄₈in (7cm) high and are shaped with rounded sides; the underneath of the base is hollow, and the words 'He played a' are slightly raised. Later types are smaller, measuring 2¹⁄₂in (6cm) in height, and have a solid base. The plinth's sides are well angled and the slogan is not in relief.

The pipe was easily lost or broken, and this has to be a consideration when valuing a Penfold or Bromford Man. What if the figurine doesn't have an aperture for the pipe or cigarette? The answer is that the hole has been filled in and painted over at some time, and it really would be the choice of the owner whether to keep it like this, or to re-open the mouth, especially if he were to find a pipe or cigarette.

The Dunlop Rubber Company also developed a composition character in the 1930s, called the Dunlop Caddie. Just as with the Penfold Man, the Dunlop

The North British 'Scottie Dog' on a rare plinth that makes it a £1,000 item instead of £800.

Caddie was played by the shop professional to encourage his playing members to play with Dunlop golf balls. There are two types of Dunlop Caddie, each with a head resembling a round, dimpled golf ball. Both figures wear a cap and a scarf and rolled-up trousers, and both carry a bag with two irons and four woods. The more common figurine measures 15–16in (38–40cm) in height. This measurement includes its green, canted, rectangular wooden base on which is inscribed: 'We Play Dunlop'. The rarer type is considerably smaller at 12¹⁄₂in (31cm) high, and bears the slogan: 'We Play Dunlop "65"'. The Dunlop 65 golf ball took its name from Henry Cotton's famous 65 at Royal George's in the second round of the1934 Open. As well as being shorter, this Dunlop Caddie has 'Dunlop 65' on the back of his head. The small-sized Dunlop Caddie is the second rarest of all the point-of-sales figurines.

In the 1940s and 1950s the North British Rubber Company commissioned the Sylvac Company to create black pottery replicas of their logo, a Scottie dog holding one of their round dimple balls in its mouth. Sylvac already made both black and white Scotties for a

Left: The Dunlop Caddie sells at auction for £700.
Middle: The Silver King Man is a rare item and sells at £4,000 plus.
Right: The Bromford Man is scarcer than the Penfold Man.

whisky company, and the mould was altered so that the dog held a golf ball. The ceramic dog so made measures 11in (28cm) high; some were presented on 2¾in (7cm) high blue plinths with the slogan: 'North British: The Choice of Champions'. These are rare. The colour of the tartan dog collar is either red or green, and some balls feature the words 'North British'.

The Silvertown Company also gave advertising figurines to golf professionals in Britain who stocked their Silver King golf balls. There are two Silver King figurines, both made from a pressed card material. The earlier type was issued some time during the 1920s and is known as the 'Silver Queen'; it is the rarest of all the figures. Dressed in a pink and black outfit with a harlequin-style pattern, and wearing a golden crown on a head that resembles a golf ball, this figure displayed a slogan on the plinth advertising 'Silver King Golf Balls'.

During the early 1930s it was replaced by a smaller Silver King figure measuring just over 14in (35cm) that was produced for the Silvertown Company by Universal Seamless Containers Ltd. It, too, has a mesh-patterned golf ball as the head, and is dressed in plus fours. This figure also wears a crown, holds a metal bulger-style club in the right hand, and is presented on a rectangular hollow wooden plinth inscribed with the words 'Silver King Golf Balls' and marked 'Patent No. 208063' on the base. This type of Silver King figure is also rare.

LEFT: By far the rarest of the advertising figures…name your price if you have one!

ABOVE: These Army & Navy paper tees are rare.

Sand Moulds and Early Tees

In the early days golfers would go to a box filled with sand, located on every teeing-up area; usually the sand would have to be dampened to make it easier to form a hand-made mould. It usually fell to the caddie to make the tee, and can be clearly seen in Sir Francis Grant's painting of John Whyte-Melville of Bannochy & Strathcainess, captain of the R & A in 1823, with his caddie.

The first development was the invention of metal tee moulds. The 'Alexander' mould was advertised as being a 'little contrivance that will recommend itself to Golfers on account of its simplicity in use, uniformity in shape of tee made and saving of sand.' The J. E. Ransome of Ipswich's (lawn-mower makers) polished brass Double Golf Tee Stamp *circa* 1900 was 'a splendid thing for making a sand tee…accurate and quick.' Priced at

1s 0d (5p), it afforded the golfer two choices of teeing heights (for either woods or irons) by using either end of the mould.

Later these moulds became more sophisticated, with springs and plungers. For example, with the Greenwood's Golf Tee Mould, sand was pushed into the mould, and when the spring-loaded top was depressed it ejected a perfectly formed sand tee: 'Any caddie can use it…makes perfect moulds…always same height …thus ensuring consistent driving.'

Although brass was the more popular medium, the British Douglas Sand Tee Gun with is cylindrical plunger was made of stainless steel, whereas the K-D tee mould *circa* 1920s, made from polished aluminium, advertised that 'you can make ten million tees of absolutely uniform height quicker and neater by hand'.

Keystone Golf Sand Tee Molders are a little more unusual in that they are made out of Bakelite, a very popular light material at the beginning of the 1910s. A trade box lid of twelve tee moulds, all in various colours, had its own helpful instructions: 'Simply scoop up some moist sand in the little cup, pack it against the side of the sandbox, press the button – and out it comes the neatest tee you ever saw. Not once, but always.'

RIGHT: A group of brass tee moulds to include a tall 'Far and Sure' mould with spring plunger mechanism. J. B. Halley & Co made the tins of enamel ball paint in 1900. In 1910 the Dunlop tin held fifteen 'New Dunlop Red Spot' bramble balls: where are they now?

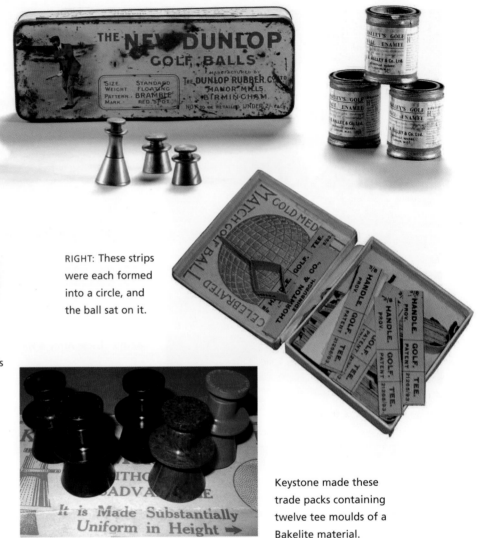

ABOVE: Both of these Ranscome brass tee moulds are stamped 'S & S' ('Safe and Sure').

RIGHT: These strips were each formed into a circle, and the ball sat on it.

Keystone made these trade packs containing twelve tee moulds of a Bakelite material.

ALTERNATIVE MATERIALS FOR TEES

In 1889 two Scots, Messrs Bloxsom and Douglas, patented the first portable golf tee formed in moulded rubber with the ball resting on three spikes. Even though a number of tee inventions followed, the sand-moulded tee remained popular, certainly with the game's traditionalists.

Tee inventions in materials ranging from rubber, metal, Bakelite, paper to wood eventually came to the fore. For example, in 1895 the first American golf patent for a tee was made from heavy paper/card. The flat piece of semi-circular paper could be formed into a cone. Colonel Bogey fully formed paper tees

came in small round boxes of twenty-five to a box. Atkinson & Griffin, gun and cycle makers in Kendal, also made similar paper tees.

A rubber tee advertised by Spalding in 1893 was a forerunner of today's wooden tee. In 1899 an American inventor called Grant came up with a tee with a wooden stem and a flexible tubular head. The first ground-piercing 'tee peg' was patented in the early 1900s in the USA. Then plain wooden tees (fifty or a hundred) were sold in cotton bags to look like pouches of tobacco.

William Lowell, a dentist, invented the all-wooden peg called the 'Reddy Tee'. It was funnel shaped and painted 'red' to stand out on the grass after the ball had

Tees have come in all sorts of size, shape and colour.

Ball Markers

Ball markers, or 'spotters', were originally called 'stymie markers', and generally fall into one of three structural types:

- **Metal coin type without a stem:** Coins may be minted for special events such as charity events. These coins with a golf theme are called 'Exonumia', which means being outside numismatics or governmental coinage.
- **Metal marker with a stem:** These first appeared in the 1920s, even though the 6in (15cm) stymie rule applied. They are made from brass or even silver, and decorated with the club, course name or logo.
- **Plastic marker with a stem:** These first appeared in the 1950s. They are made from hard plastic and often sport a slogan or just the name of the club.

The merits of collecting ball markers are that they are durable, often attractive, and inexpensive, and they are an archive of one's personal golfing memories. They are also easy and cheap to display.

been hit. Woolworth's stocked it, and Walter Hagen endorsed it. It couldn't fail. By 1930 there had been over 550 golf tee patents filed in the UK and the USA.

Although the basic tee concept has remained unchanged, there were many packaging variations, such as packs of plastic tees being sold in 'matchboxes', often with printed scorecards printed on their reverse. There were all sorts of shapes, such as carrot, funnel, goblet, classic and trumpets, this last being basically the shape of the tee that is still popular today.

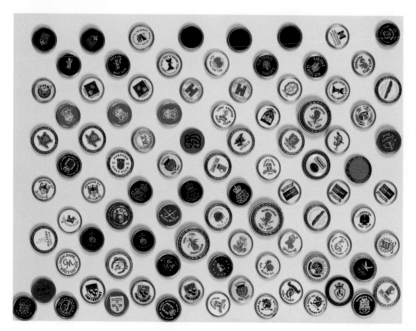

A selection of ball markers: bright, and so easy to display.

Two 1800 woods. *Left:* An extremely rare McEwan long spoon, *circa* 1800.
Right: An early nineteenth-century McEwan putter, *circa* 1820.

GOLF CLUBS, PATENT CLUBS AND SUNDAY CLUBS

The Oldest Set of Golf Clubs in the World

Although golf as we know it was played as long ago as the late fifteenth century, there are sadly no surviving examples of early golf clubs. However, a small number have survived from the mid to late 1700s and early 1800s. These are all in private collections, museums and golf clubs such as Royal Blackheath. Of course, who knows what might still turn up! The 'Troon' clubs dating to the late seventeenth century or early eighteenth century are the oldest existing set of clubs in the world. They were discovered in 1898 in a cupboard in a house in Hull wrapped in a newspaper dated 1741. They were later presented to the (Royal) Troon Golf Club by Adam Wood, a past captain, and are currently on display at the British Golf Museum in St Andrews.

The heads are decorated with a crown and the initials 'C' and 'T' or an 'I', and some have suggested that these refer to the Stuart kings. Their wooden heads are shaped with a blunted toe, and are redolent of the clubs shown being held in the painting of the Blackheath Golfers, as discussed in Chapter 4 (*see* p. 83).

Long Nose Clubs

Until the introduction of the compact, convex-faced Bulger heads in the 1880s, the design of wooden golf clubs was more or less constant. Wooden clubs had long, slender heads up to 5½in (14cm) in length, with a long neck that was attached to the shaft by a spliced joint. These were called scared (as in frightened) neck, long nose clubs, and endured for over 300 years.

There is something wonderful about these elegantly crafted, wooden-headed golf clubs made from a variety of woods including holly, apple, beech and, less commonly, hornbeam.

The term 'long nose' described the elongated tear drop-shaped club head with its slim neck and shallow face. Woods made during the feathery ball era (up to the 1860s) were rarely ever more than 1in (2.5cm) in depth; in the gutta-percha period (1850s to the end of the nineteenth century) the clubface became slightly deeper, and woods were made with a thicker neck to withstand the rigors of the harder ball material. The most widely used timbers before the 1800s were all British (Scottish), and included whitethorn (hawthorn), apple, pear and beech. With the advent of the harder gutty ball, new timbers were experimented with, such as dogwood, holly and hornbeam – but by far the most popular was the durable beech wood. Persimmon was introduced in the late1890s, just as the ball was about to undergo its next big development from a gutta-percha to a rubber-cored ball.

Generally, scared neck woods pre-1900 were made from beech, and after 1900 socket neck woods were made in persimmon. The scare was an old joinery term (scarf), and was the way in which the long tapering shaft, cut at the thinner neck end with a splice of approximately 4½ to 6in (11 to 12.5cm) in length, fitted a contra-splice on the socket of the club head. Adding lead to the cavity at the back of the head gave the club its balance or feel.

A piece of horn, originally ram's horn and later cattle horn (sometimes white in colour), was pegged or dowled to the underneath of the leading edge, and this afforded the club some protection from contact with the ground at impact. There was only one type of sheep in Scotland that really had a big enough horn to make long enough pieces: the black-faced sheep. All the

Listing grip sewn with red thread.

Ash shaft

A seventeenth century spur iron.

Hosel

Sharp tooth nicking

Head of nail

Head made from wrought iron

Crease

Spur

horns made from this animal were black or nearly black. The crown or top of the head was often stamped with the maker's name, and in later years the retailer's name, too.

The shaft was originally made from ash, and sometimes hazel. In time, various other woods were used, including lemon wood and hickory; from Central America came greenheart and lancewood. Hickory proved the most resilient, and soon became the most widely used shaft material. Danga wood (a trade mark) was also used in the 1930s when good hickory was running out.

Strips of hide leather or sheepskin were fitted to grip the club with. Between this and the shaft was fitted an underlisting, usually made from upholsterer's felt or blankets, also known as 'stuff' or 'rind'. As the ball became harder the underlisting became quite thick, to protect golfers' hands from the sting of impact. However, the rubber core ball, introduced in the early 1900s, absorbed much of the impact shock; also the 'Vardon grip' became more popular and replaced the two-handed grip, and as a result golf club grips became quite thin.

The face of the club would be crafted and lofted to deliver different trajectories. Later the club maker would repair face damage with a leather or – though very rarely – gutta-percha insert. Inserts were relatively easy to fit, secured by glue and tiny pegs or pins, and were light and cheap and reasonably effective: better to prolong the life of the club than chop down another tree and make a new one – golfers, being what they

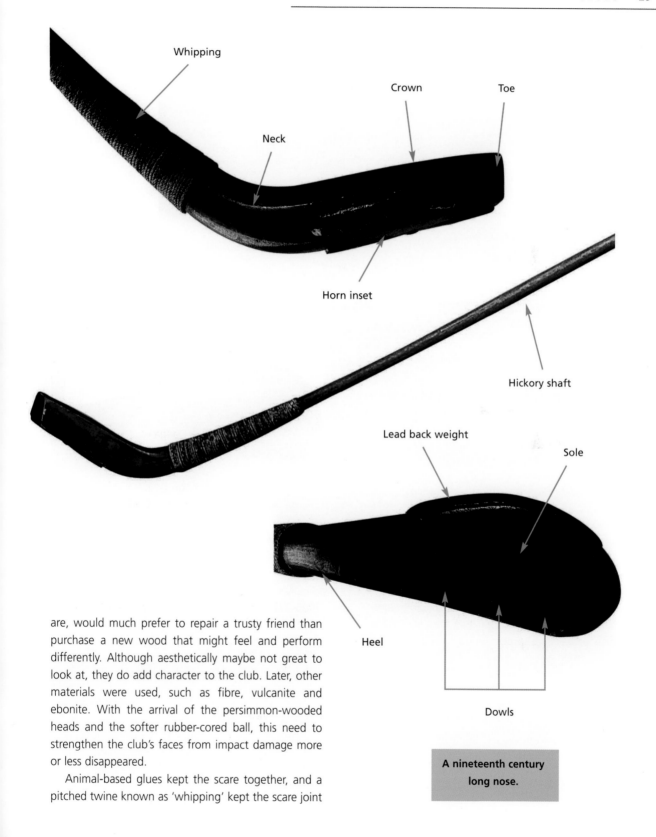

Whipping

Crown

Toe

Neck

Horn inset

Hickory shaft

Lead back weight

Sole

Heel

Dowls

are, would much prefer to repair a trusty friend than purchase a new wood that might feel and perform differently. Although aesthetically maybe not great to look at, they do add character to the club. Later, other materials were used, such as fibre, vulcanite and ebonite. With the arrival of the persimmon-wooded heads and the softer rubber-cored ball, this need to strengthen the club's faces from impact damage more or less disappeared.

Animal-based glues kept the scare together, and a pitched twine known as 'whipping' kept the scare joint

A nineteenth century long nose.

The standard practice was to use three pegs in the horn. This one has four.

SOME EARLY CLUB MAKERS

● **Hugh Philp (1782–1856):** Known as the Stradivarius of all club makers, Philp hand crafted the most beautiful looking wood heads. A Philp club characteristically had a long narrow face and a slender elegant neck, and was perfectly balanced. In 1819 he was appointed club maker to the Society of St Andrews (later the R & A). He was renowned as a fine golfer himself, and won many a wager over the St Andrews links. He also took on apprentices, as was the norm, and passed on his club-making skills. Robert Forgan, his nephew, joined him in 1852.

● **The McEwans:** The most famous family of club makers, six generations from James of Leith in 1770 to Peter in more recent times in the late 1800s. Douglas moved to Musselburgh in 1847, and married into the famous Gourlay feather ball-making family. It was said of a McEwan club: 'Theirs was an art, not a trade.' There was little difference in the shape of clubs produced by the first generation of club makers, such as James McEwan, right up until the arrival of the new, hard, gutta-percha ball in the middle of the nineteenth century. Then these beautiful long-nose woods had to be strengthened in the areas that absorbed the most stress – namely the face and the neck – although their overall head shape did not change.

A short spoon circa 1786 stamped with the name 'J. McEwan' and the thistle; this is one of only three such clubs. The 'McEwan' feather golf ball was made in 1836, probably by the Gourlays, to mark the death of Peter McEwan and his son, James, who died on the same day in April that year.

● **Robert Forgan (1824–1900):** Hugh Philp's nephew and apprentice, Forgan soon became one of the most significant and prolific club makers of his time. His reputation was so good that the Prince of Wales (later King Edward VII) commissioned Forgan to make him a set of clubs. Accordingly, pre-1901 Forgan clubs are usually stamped with the Prince of Wales plume symbol, and post-1902 clubs with a crown symbol. Forgan dispensed with the crown symbol when the new monarch George V came to the throne in 1909. His premium quality clubs usually have 'R Forgan & Son, St Andrews Selected' stamped into the shaft just below the grip.

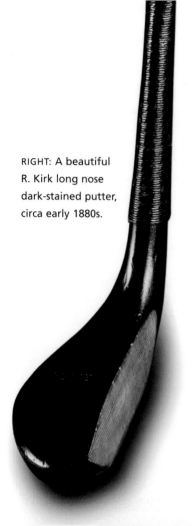

RIGHT: A beautiful R. Kirk long nose dark-stained putter, circa early 1880s.

RIGHT: There were several attempts to arrive at a stronger way of joining the head and the shaft. This Army & Navy club has a frontal splice and is quite rare.

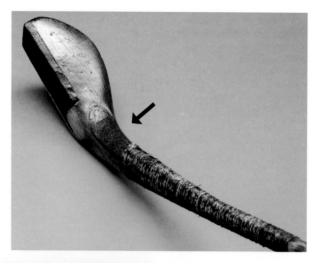

LEFT: This rare putter is only the fourth long nose presentation club to be recorded. It sold at auction for just under £7,500 in 2005.

LEFT: A selection of long nose woods. From left: Robert Anderson; John Butchart; Dickson; Frank Doleman; Tom Dunn; and two George Forresters.

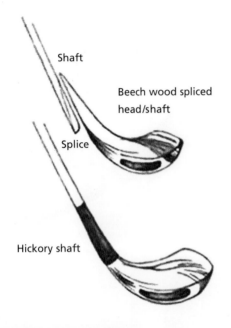

Shaft

Beech wood spliced head/shaft

Splice

Hickory shaft

The shaft is glued to the head by a 'scare joint' and secured with a pitched thread whipping 4.5in (11cm) long. Scare is derived from the word 'scarf', meaning a flat, over-lapping joint.

tightly in place and protected the adhesive that could dissolve if attacked by water. The whipping was 'water-proofed' by hot bitumen, and then varnished; if applied properly, it would start approximately ½in (1.5cm) above the top join, and finish ½in above the bottom join, leaving ½in at the tip of the shaft showing. Usually the older or earlier the club, the thicker the whipping thread used.

SOME NINETEENTH-CENTURY CLUB MAKERS

A popular theme is to collect long nose clubs that were made by winners of the Open, such as Willie Park Sr, who won the first championship in 1860, Tom Morris,

LEFT: This Hugh Philp driver is about as good as it gets for condition and collectability.

LEFT: This is the Philp putter used by young Tom Morris to win the 1872 Open.

BELOW: A close-up of the Hugh Philp putter.

Andrew Strath, and in latter years the prolific Auchterlonies. This theme can be developed to collecting the long nose clubs that were actually used to win an Open. However, this would be limited to those with serious money and plenty of patience, because such clubs are few and far between. Any club of this type must have a letter of provenance to prove its origins.

COLLECTORS' NOTES

● Early wooden clubs: do not be put off by face repairs such as leather face inserts, as these can enhance the creditability of the club and its value.
● Do look at the horn sole insert. The hooked or toed-in face is often filed back, leaving the horn narrower at the toe end than at the heel end. This can seriously devalue the club.
● Regarding the scare: look for the tell-tale ¹/₂in (13mm) tongue that is exposed at the bottom; if it is not visible it usually means that the whipping has been replaced incorrectly or has been done to hide a poorly refitted shaft.
● The two areas of the club that can be renovated without affecting the value of the club too much are the whipping and, to a lesser extent, the grip.
● If you come across a club stamped with both 'Philp' and 'Forgan', it is one of some 200 persimmon-headed putters made by Forgan & Son in 1906 to mark the fiftieth anniversary of Philp's death. These are rare and collectable.

The Early Iron-Headed Clubs

Blacksmiths began to craft the earliest iron-headed clubs during the mid-1700s. They are so rare (and expensive, often selling for sums in excess of £50,000) that they very seldom come on to the market. The majority of surviving clubs, such as square toe irons and spur irons, are in museums, established golf club collections and private collections.

The spur toe family are the earliest of the irons, and the 'spur' on the toe was provided to help the club cut through the grass, especially when it was long. The characteristics of such a club would include a 1in- (2.5cm-) diameter ash shaft and a 5¹/₂in (14cm) hosel. By the mid-1600s the square toe iron had lost its spur.

An ancient spur toe iron that would have been made by an armourer or blacksmith in or around 1680. The 'spur' is the protrusion at the bottom of the left edge of the head.

There are only six or so known examples to exist (one was in the Troon collection); the majority have deep blades and are known as 'heavy' irons as opposed to 'light' irons. As it is believed that they are all accounted for, and it is unlikely that a new find will be made, we will move on.

The 1840s to the late 1880s has become a golden period for iron club collectors because the irons, whilst a little crude, are quite stylish with their thick grips, thick hosels (the join at the neck of the blade between the hosel and the top of the head), and wide hosel creases. The top of the hosel, where the shaft is fitted, is often 'decorated' with deep knurling, and about 1in (2.5cm) down will be found a smoothed-off square peg or rivet to keep the club head secure.

During this period very few types of iron were used, mainly woods, so there was no 'set in stone' characteristic for each iron. That is why collecting from this era is so exciting, as you may well find an iron that does not fit into a certain category.

TYPES OF CLUB

The following clubs are examples of the type normally found:

● **Cleek:** Used for long distance hitting. The narrow, long, almost parallel head would produce a low,

Left: A rare mid-eighteenth-century square toe iron with a 5in (13cm) stout hosel nailed in line with the blade and an ash shaft.
Right: An early to mid-nineteenth-century lofting iron with a 5in hosel and well dished face.

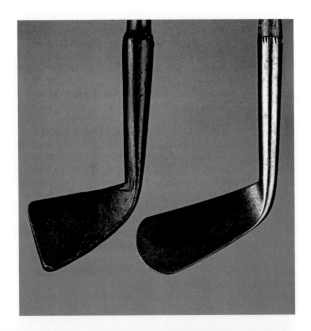

boring shot. The length of the club is similar to a No. 1 iron today, measuring 40in (100cm) in length, and with a loft of 17 to 20 degrees.

- **The lofting iron:** Shorter in length than a cleek, with an oversized head and loft of 35 to 40 degrees. As the name implies, it was used to get the ball out of hazards on to the green, and was used as a sand iron to get out of bunkers.

- **General iron:** Similar in head size and looks as a lofter, with a good, long, thick hosel but with less loft, comparable to a modern No. 5 iron at around

CLUB NAMES BEFORE NUMBERED CLUBS

- **Baffy:** Wooden club to play lofting shots. *See* **Spoon** below.

- **Driver or play club:** Used to propel (drive) the ball from the teeing-up area. The characteristics of a play club would include a long, usually 43–46in (110–115cm), tapering, flexible shaft, and an elegant head with around 10 degrees of face loft that produced a low, boring shot. The grassed driver had a little more face loft to get the ball more easily airborne.

- **Spoon:** Mainly used to hit shots from the fairway. There were several types, known as the long spoon, middle spoon and short spoon. They all had a similar face loft of 15 to 17 degrees, but their shafts varied in length, as their names suggest; the long spoon at 42in (105cm) produced the longest distance, and the middle and short spoons, as progressively shorter, would help to deliver more control from tricky, tight lies. As spoons were used more frequently during a game of golf and tended to become easily damaged, there are fewer around today than drivers from the same era. The baffing spoon was more like today's No. 5 wood: it had

more loft than any other spoon, and was used to produce a shorter, high shot to the green.

- **Wooden niblick:** With its shortened, stiff shaft and short stubby head, and its well lofted, spooned face, it was ideal to dislodge the ball from a tight lie, hollow or rut. This was one of the first wooden clubs made more or less redundant by the 1890s and replaced by irons. A rare and valuable club if found today.

- **Brassie:** The 1890s saw the introduction of the 'brassie' wood with its protected, full brass sole plate. Having a little more loft and being slightly shorter than a driver, it was easier to use both off the tee and from the fairway when long distance was required.

- **Putters:** The long-nosed putter was much shorter in length, between 35 to 38in (87 to 95cm), and more upright in comparison to a play club. The driving putter had a very stiff shaft and was used to execute a low running shot into the wind, or along bone-hard fairways from some distance away from the green.

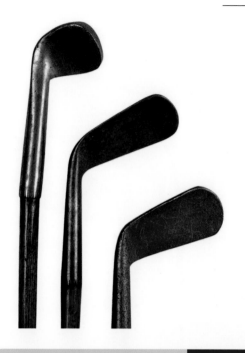

Left: A late eighteenth- /early nineteenth-century thick blade lofting iron with 4¹/₂in (11cm) hosel and stout ash shaft.
Middle: An early nineteenth-century cleek with 5in (13cm) hosel and deep nicking.
Right: A nineteenth-century lofting iron with 5in hosel and curved blade.

30 degrees of loft, helping to produce a longer, higher shot.

● **Track or rut iron:** Shortest of all the irons in length and fitted with a stiff shaft, this was a real trouble-shooting club. The head was designed to extract the ball from the many cart tracks or ruts found on the course. In these early times, the ball had to be played from where it lay, as the 'pick and drop' rule had not come into force. Early track irons were almost circular in head shape, and quite often had a

BUYER BEWARE

PLAY A PROVISIONAL BALL

✳ Is the wood stained black or a similar dark colour? Maybe it has been re-coloured to hide a crack or other head damage. It is near impossible to conceal such damage when the wood is light coloured.

✳ Check the shafts and make sure they look properly tapered and not too thick.

✳ Eddie Davis was a famous club maker who resided in Westward Ho! during the mid to late twentieth century. He made several replica long-nosed clubs, and these are usually stamped with his name. But there are fakes, too, and these range from very good to really poor. It is of course the first category that is the worry, because they are usually sold to unsuspecting collectors for high prices. More often than not it is a case of greed dispelling common sense and drowning out those ringing alarm bells telling you that maybe there is something not quite right with the club. The buyer always wants to believe that what he is buying is the real thing.

✳ Suspicion should be centred to the grip, as these are very difficult to age, and in some instances fake clubs are sold without grips; check the age of the horn, and if you can't tell the difference between ram's horn and the more common cattle's horn, get an expert to do so.

✳ Check the type of wood used, for example club makers were not using persimmon in the eighteenth century.

✳ Look at the maker's letters on the crown of the club head: have they been unevenly or individually stamped into the wood? If they have, something is wrong, because all the good club makers had their own stamps made so that with a swipe of the hammer the whole name was reproduced into the wood.

✳ Finally have a look at the angle of the name: it should be angled slightly towards the toe of the head when looking down at the club at the address, and not straight across, as is often the case with fakes.

An early rut iron with 5in (13cm) hosel and ash shaft.

Left: A late eighteenth-, early nineteenth-century thick bladed lofting iron with 4½in (11cm) hosel.
Middle: An early nineteenth-century cleek with 5in (13cm) hosel and deep nicking.
Right: An early nineteenth-century lofting iron with 5in hosel and curved blade.

OPPOSITE: A selection of mainly mid to late nineteenth-century lofting irons.

cupped or concave thick face, and a sturdy, round, parallel hosel; they would feel quite heavy.

Towards the 1890s the iron became much more refined, with a larger, slimmer head without the concave face; it became known as the 'rut niblick', which became the forerunner of the niblick and modern-day wedge. Although this club was meant to help get the ball airborne quickly, it can often be found with a relatively straight face. As there was no definitive model for this type of iron, the loft on the face could vary by as much as 10–15 degrees.

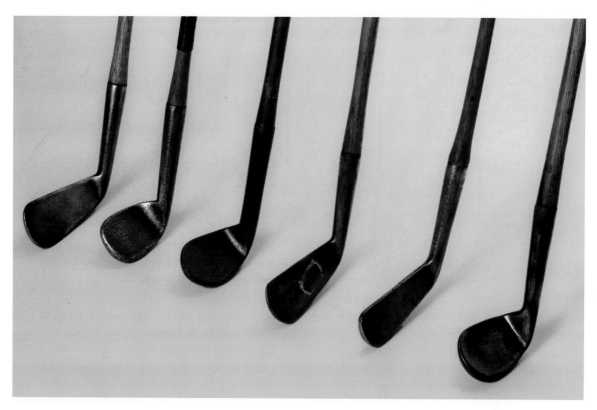

Later Long Nose, Transitional and Bulger Clubs

The next development in wooden clubs came about in 1850, when golf adopted the new golf ball that was made from a hard gutta-percha material. These balls caused havoc with the elegant long-nosed clubs, and breakages became more and more common. The shape of the club head by necessity had to develop. Firstly, the long nose woods became deeper in the face and thicker in the neck, and by the 1880s a new, sturdier shape had evolved: known as 'transitional', or late long nose, the head was now quite a bit shorter than the earlier long nose heads, but still retained the thicker neck and deeper face.

These are very popular with newer collectors because although they resemble late long nose clubs, they cost only a fraction of the price of an earlier long nose wood. Transitional clubs are also important for those who want to collect one club from each significant era, or to display how the wooden clubs evolved.

During the middle 1880s there was a real explosion of changing golf club head shape, and the long nose was soon to become extinct. A club known as the bulger was coming on to the scene, and was about to herald a completely new design. Unlike any style of head before it, the bulger had a round or convex face. It was found to produce a more accurate shot with less side spin through the interaction of a round ball with a round face. Together with a much more symmetrically round head and thick neck, this wood was far more robust and lasted much longer than its predecessors. Towards 1900 the bulger became even more refined as the head became smaller and the neck slimmer. Remarkably this head shape – other than for the change in shaft fitting to be explained later – stayed, in larger and smaller versions, right up until the 1980s.

A Summary of the Development of the Wooden Driving Club

Long nose pre-1860: To measure, hold the club in your left hand with the front of the face looking towards you at near eye level. Measure from the

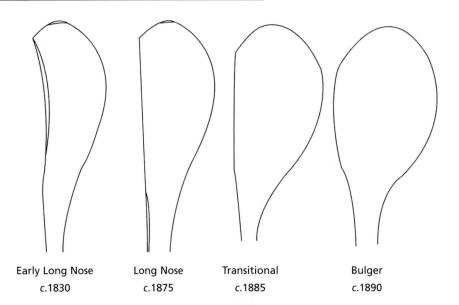

Early Long Nose
c.1830

Long Nose
c.1875

Transitional
c.1885

Bulger
c.1890

outside of the neck to the very end of the toe in a straight line across the face.

The head measures 5 to 6in (13 to 15cm) in length. The shallow face, 1in (2.5cm) deep, has a definite toe-to-heel curvature, giving a slight concave look; a slim scare neck fitted with around 5in (13cm) of tarred, coarse binding or thread; the shaft, depending on the loft of the club, will be between 42 and 46in (105 and 115cm) long, and will be fitted with a sheep or hide grip with cloth underlisting.

Long nose pre-1880: Heads are now 4¼ to 5in (11 to 13in) long, and there is no longer a hook or concave face. The face is deeper at 1¼in (3cm). The neck is now thicker and wider (the wood is now mainly beech, rather than thorn), while the scare neck thread is still the same at 5in (13cm). The grip has

CLUB NAMES BEFORE NUMBERED CLUBS

Cleek: The straightest face, longest hitting iron.

Driving iron/long iron: More loft than a cleek, similar to a modern No. 3 iron.

Mid iron: More loft than a long iron, similar to a modern No. 4 iron.

Mashie: A middle distance iron, loft similar to a modern No. 5 or 6 iron.

Lofting iron: An early form of mashie niblick with an oversized head club, to play high lofted shots on to the green. Also used as a sand iron for getting the ball out of bunkers or similar hazards.

Spade mashie/deep face mashie: Loft similar to a modern No. 6 or 7 iron.

Mashie niblick: Loft similar to a No. 8 or 9 iron.

Rut iron/track iron: Earliest, short, well lofted iron with a small, near-round head, to extricate the ball from rut and cart tracks.

Rut niblick: After the rut iron with a slightly larger head and before the niblick.

Niblick: Later model with a larger head than the rut niblick, with loft similar to a wedge/sand iron.

Jigger: Similar loft to a mid iron, used for long shots and pitch and run shots around the green.

Sammy: Same as the jigger, but with a rounded back.

become thicker with more padding or underlisting under it.

Late long nose/transitional 1880s: Heads are shorter and broader than any long nose, but can vary in dimensions, as many clubmakers were experimenting with head shapes. Grips quite often appear to be oversized or well padded for the double-handed grip, and to afford more protection for the hands at impact from the hard ball.

Bulger mid-1880s: This period now shows a very definite change to the new shape of head design. Not only is the head becoming oval in shape, the face now shows a bulge or convex look. The neck is often very thick and wide, but it does slim down again towards 1902, when the rubber-cored ball comes into use. Grips are generally at their thickest during this period, and are well padded with layers of cloth underlisting. The neck whipping is still the same length as the early long nose clubs, at around 5in (13cm).

Later Irons and Cleek Marks

The iron club developed with the advent of the gutta-percha ball in the 1850s, and soon there were more specific clubs for certain shots.

In 1860, F. & A. Carrick of Musselburgh became one of the first blacksmiths to make forged iron-headed clubs. Their cleek mark (or maker's mark) was simply a

A selection of wooden clubs showing the easily recognizable head shapes of the nineteenth-century form of long nose, transitional and bulger.

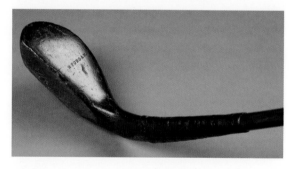

A Robert Forgan, dark-stained, long nose putter, circa 1885.

cross symbol. (Carricks are cornerstone clubs of a good club collection.) A contemporary of theirs was John Gray of Prestwick, who had begun forging irons a couple of years before the Carricks and was active until the 1880s. He stamped his clubs 'J. Gray', 'Jn. Gray' or 'Gray'. His clubs are very collectable.

During the period 1880–1910, the better Scottish club makers, such as Tom Stewart, Robert Condie and George Nicoll, who were then three of the most prolific club makers in Scotland (the world), would supply other club professionals with their club heads, for them to shaft and grip themselves. At the beginning of the

THE CADDIE AND THE AUTOMATON CADDIE

Until the explosion in popularity of golf during the 1880s and 1890s, no well-to-do player would have played without a caddie carrying his or her clubs for them. Caddies, such as the one seen in the *Blackheath Golfers* painting, originally carried the seven or so clubs as a bundle under their arms. A development was the introduction of canvas carrying bags that made it easier for the caddies – although soon the number of golfers far outnumbered the number of caddies. A compromise solution was needed to replace the human caddie.

In 1893, J. Osmond, an 'inventor and patentee' based at the Thornhill works in Lee in London, patented his golf bag invention: the 'Osmond's Patent Automaton Caddie'. The word 'caddie' in this context referred to the bag itself, and not the person carrying it. It comprised a canvas bag attached to a wooden frame. The wooden legs at the front, when released, kept the bag and frame off the fairway. The legs opened out automatically when the lower end was placed on the ground, and folded up close when it was lifted for carrying (a device that is still used today by many bag manufacturers, and one that is often marketed as being a new invention!).

The Automaton Caddie was carried by a sturdy handle, but for the equivalent of an extra 10p, golfers at the turn of the twentieth century could have a leather sling that 'enabled the bag and frame to be carried by the player on the shoulder'.

When new, the price for the Model No. 1 (for ladies) was the equivalent of 62p, and Model No. 2 (for men)

Left: A Bussey patent caddie circa 1890s.
Right: An Osmond's patent the 'Automaton Caddie', circa 1890s.

was available for the equivalent of 75p. Automaton Caddies remain popular with golfing memorabilia collectors because they can then realistically showcase their old clubs. Always check for damage, especially to the delicate moving legs, and for the dreaded woodworm.

---

twentieth century it has been estimated that ten to twelve cleek makers accounted for 90 per cent of the heads forged.

Before supplying to other professionals, they stamped or branded each head as theirs. These marks became known as 'cleek marks', and of course denoted who was the original maker of the club head. The professional – or quite often the sports store that they were sold through – would also have their name or brand model added to the head. Some iron heads carry an amazing amount of information on the back from

these different sources; a similar situation would be the way in which precious metals are hall marked.

Tom Stewart's mark was an upturned clay pipe mark, and because in the 1920s he made clubs for personal use by Bobby Jones, Tom Stewart clubs remain popular collectables, especially in America. Robert Condie, St Andrews, was a well respected 'cleek maker' during the early 1880s, and the firm continued to make clubs into the 1930s. Look for the Condie 'flower' mark and the single and double 'fern': the fern marks always sell with a premium. The J. & D. Clark proprietors had learned

If you want a Good Club, get a Good Golfer to make it.

GOLF CLUBS.

	Ordinary Clubs with Hickory, Shafts. each.	Extra Finished Selected Hickory, Greenheart, Lancewood, &c. each.	Boys' Clubs. each
	s. d.	s. d.	s. d.
Drivers,	4 6	5 0	3 6
Long Spoons,	4 6	5 0	3 6
Mid Spoons,	4 6	5 0	3 6
Short Spoons,	4 6	5 0	3 6
Putters,	4 6	5 0	3 6
Brassy Spoons,	5 6	6 0	4 6
Brassy Niblicks,	5 6	6 0	4 6
Brassy Bulgers,	6 0	6 6	
Cleeks,	5 6	6 0	4 6
Irons,	5 6	6 0	4 6
Iron Niblicks,	5 6	6 0	4 6

Extra Clubs

Driving Cleeks,	5 6	6 0
Putting Cleeks,	5 6	6 0
Driving Irons,	5 6	6 0
Lofting Irons,	5 6	6 0
Iron Putters,	5 6	6 0
Mashies,	5 6	6 0
Driving Putters,	4 6	5 0
Baffing Spoons,	4 6	5 0
Club Walking Sticks,	4 6	4 6

Bulger Golf Clubs, by the Inventor, W. PARK, Jun., 5s. each.
LADIES' GOLF CLUBS.—An Assortment of Ladies' Clubs is kept in Stock.
LEFT-HANDED CLUBS are also kept in Stock.
Park's Patent Compressed Unbreakable Wood Golf Clubs,
Drivers, 7s. 6d. each ; Brasseys, 8s. 6d. each.
Park's Patent Lofter (Over 17,000 Sold).
Park's Patent Driving Cleeks (Over 8000 Sold).
Park's Special Patent Putting Cleek—PRICE 7s. 6d. each—(Over 5000 Sold).

GOLF BALLS.

For Cash with Order only.

Park's Special (Patented),	1s. each.	12s. per doz.
Best "Silvertown," No. 1 (own painting),	1s. „	12s. „
A-1 Ball,	1s. „	12s. „
Old Balls sent to be made up,	3d. „	8s. „
Old Balls sent to be re-painted	2d. „	2s. „

WM. PARK, JUN.,
(Champion Golfer, 1887, 1889),
GOLF CLUB MAKER,
MUSSELBURGH, N.B.,
AND
6 SOUTH ST. ANDREW STREET, EDINBURGH.

DETERMINING THE ERA OF YOUR SCARED NECK WOOD

A great deal of confusion surrounds the period when the long nose became semi-long nose, which developed into the transitional, that quickly became the early bulger. As so many makers were trying to produce their own style of progressive head development during the 1880s until the acceptance of the bulger in the mid-1890s, many wooden-headed clubs do not seem to fit into an exact type, and many seem to include characteristics from more than one type of head. For example, it is possible to find a club that looks semi-long nose with a 'bulged' face, or to find a bulger with a straight face. Just remember that this was an era of great change, and so it will be possible to find many hybrid-type clubs. Of course, that just adds to the excitement of collecting, and you might just come across a club head design that is unique and hence valuable.

LEFT: 1894: What more could the aspiring golfer wish for?

their trade from Willie Park, and they produced quality clubs between the 1890s and early 1900s. Their cleek mark was no more than their name in a circle. Charles Gibson of Westward Ho! didn't start to use a traditional cleek mark until the early 1910s, when he stamped his clubs with a rampant stallion mark. William Gibson of Kinghorn, Fife, Scotland was a prodigious club maker in the late nineteenth century and early part of the twentieth century: he used his now world-famous mark, a five-pointed star.

The faces of early iron clubs remained smooth, and it was not until the 1890s that face marking was first introduced. At this time it was discovered that an indented, patterned face helped the aerodynamics of the golf ball. Markings were at first crudely hand-punched dots; later when marked by machines they became much more uniform. Manufacturers experimented with many different types of face markings until the horizontal lines that we see on today's irons became the norm in the late 1920s. So take a close look at the face when trying to date the age of a club, because a smooth, hand-punched, or machine face will provide an indication of its era.

Some of the most interesting clubs from this period were the oversized niblicks. Cochrane produced a Super Giant Niblick, the head of which measured 4½ x 6½in (11 x 16cm), virtually the size of a small saucepan. The more common are the Mammoth and Giant Niblick produced by many of the best makers of the day, including Hendry and Bishop, Ben Sayers, Winton and Gibson. Other similar but smaller-headed clubs include the Junior Mammoth, the Dreadnought and the Jumbo

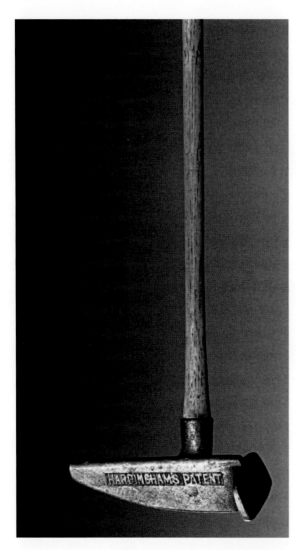

ABOVE: The patented brass-headed Arthur Hardingham putter with its rear bar projection could be mistaken for a lethal weapon.

ABOVE RIGHT: An extremely unusual and rare combination wood with brass-framed fruitwood head, wooden face and hickory shaft.

RIGHT: An extremely rare, mallet-headed putter with beech head, tapered brass sole plate, lead counterweight and hickory shaft.

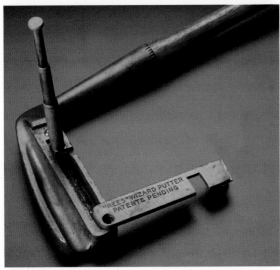

LEFT: A possibly unique combination wood, formed by a brass-framed wooden head with a hatched face, lead counterweight and hickory shaft.

BELOW: Rees Wizard putter with movable alignment extension in its back.

Niblicks. In collecting terms, the bigger the head, the rarer it is, and so is worth the most.

Patented Woods and Irons

In the 1890s and early 1900s, Great Britain produced many great engineers and inventors. Even the traditional game of golf had its fair share of new inventions that were to become important landmarks in the development of the game. These inventors came from all walks of life and included aristocrats, qualified engineers and existing golf professionals. Patent clubs would have an unusual characteristic that would be the subject of a patent, since patents afford a degree of protection against another party stealing the patented idea. In Britain the patent would last a maximum of twenty years from the date the application was filed. The term 'patent letters' showed that a patent had been granted to protect against imitators.

The majority of these inventors and designers attempted to create clubs that would hit the ball further, stop it more quickly, or putt it straighter. Some of them explored the materials used, some concentrated on shapes and designs. Traditionally made wooden clubs with their asymmetrical shape were difficult to manufacture easily; they were also labour-intensive and relatively costly to produce. So club makers and engineers began asking why golf clubs had to be made from wood, and why the club head had to be rounded? Why did it have to be attached to the shaft, rather than inserted into the head? And why did golfers have to carry several different clubs when one could be used to play a variety of shots?

The market for unusual and patent clubs made at the end of the nineteenth and beginning of the twentieth centuries remains a strong one.

SOME PATENT CLUBS IN DETAIL
Thomas Johnston patented **the very first golf club** in 1876. It would be a further thirteen years before the second patent was to be issued. At first glance the club's head appears to be made from a dark wood typical of late nineteenth-century long nose clubs; however, Johnston used vulcanite, a vulcanized India rubber, to make the heads of the club. Why? If it was

ABOVE: A fine example of a Johnston spoon that was made from vulcanite instead of wood.

RIGHT: The Claude Johnson patent Pattern B. Its shape is redolent of the metal clubs that were introduced in the 1990s, some 100 years later.

successful Johnston knew that by mass-producing them they would be cheaper than the traditional hand-crafted long nose clubs; they would be uniform in their construction because the vulcanite was poured into moulds; being made of hardened rubber they would not suffer from damage normally caused to the wood by wet weather; and finally, being more resilient than 'hard' wood they would be less punishing on the golf ball. What could go wrong? Drivers, spoons and putters were all made, but fewer than ten in total have sur-vived. Obviously, for some reason golfers did not like them very much.

There are also fewer than ten surviving **Claude Johnson patent drivers**. An important feature was how Johnson joined the head to the shaft – the shaft was inserted and secured in a brass ferrule that was embedded in the heel of the head. It has a distinct 'D'-shaped head reminiscent in style to the first titanium-headed drivers of the 1990s. Another feature of the Johnson club was its variable weighting system: metal half-inch (1cm) discs could be placed in a hole in the top of the head. If the club was too heavy, then the metal discs could be replaced with similar-shaped cork discs. A screwed down brass plate kept the weights in place.

Today the value of this club can be adversely affected if these weights have been lost.

Walter H. Dalrymple's hammer-headed golf club was patented in 1893 (No.16,148). The Baronet of North Berwick, Sir Walter Hamilton Dalrymple, began designing and patenting 'double-faced hammer-head-ed' clubs in 1892. He was a good player, and was keen to develop a range of clubs to create better ball striking. He believed that the hammer shape of the club head would give the timber 'greater strength and durability'. There were three different models. The 'bleek' was a combination of an iron club and a cleek: 'The two faces and the sole may be formed as one brass casting, the central part being wood; two screws kept the club together.' Another feature was that the wooden shaft was fitted through the centre of the club head in an attempt to get better 'accuracy of aim' and 'greater driving power'. Today this patent is a highly collectable and valuable golf club.

Breaking drivers at the neck had been a constant problem with scared neck woods, and so a great leap forward was the patent that 'invented' the socket neck wood. A number of well known club makers had begun experimenting with the shaft going directly into the

A selection of collectable putters and irons.
Far left: A G. H. Harrison patented croquet-style putter with squared ends.
Second left: A Charles H. Seely forked hosel patent iron.
Centre: A Pro-Swing practice club circa 1935.

head, among them George Forrester, Charles Gibson and Ben Sayers. But the winner was **Robert Anderson** who received a patent for a **socket neck wood** in 1891. While not all golfers embraced the new patent during its early years, it soon proved to be a popular design, and by the beginning of the 1900s became the standard way in which to attach the head to the shaft, and has remained so to the present day.

Also in 1891 **Thomas Carruthers of Edinburgh** patented his **through-bore iron-head cleek**. The Carruthers' patent featured a short thick hosel with a through-bore hole that allowed the shaft to be fitted to within 1/8in (3mm) of the sole. The weight in the hosel was therefore reduced, which in turn enhanced the

This Carruthers' advertisement was published in 1892.

ABOVE: A selection of putters.
Left: A patented J. K. Garner billiard-style, two disc-faced brass putter circa 1904.
Second from right: An Otto Hackbarth patented forked hosel putter.

LEFT: A close-up of the Carruthers' patented socket.

balance of the head and the playability of the club. By the early 1910s the through-bore iron head had become very popular in America with golf club manufacturers such as Spalding and MacGregor, using the patent under licence. Some manufacturers such as Callaway still use this method today in their iron-head design.

OTHER PATENTED CLUBS

Willie Park's patent No. 5,042 of 1889 was actually the **first for a golf club**, rather than a part or variation of an existing design. His patented iron had a short, compact blade with a flattish toe, a concave face and a long, heavy hosel that was very different to the long-bladed lofting irons in vogue at the time.

George Forrester's concentric or **centre-balanced cleeks and irons** were patented under No. 12,524 in 1890. Instead of the blade being a flat iron bar, Forrester shaped the back so the area behind the sweet spot was thicker than the areas around the heel and toe; the blade was thickest at its sole.

Robert L. Urquhart is known today for his **adjustable clubs** made under patents No. 8,176 (1892)

The Jean Gassiat putter in the centre remains popular; the club second from the right is a rare Thomas Johnston-patented long spoon made from vulcanite *circa* 1876.

and No. 9,419 (1893). Scotsman Robert Urquhart was a keen golfer and a member of the Honourable Company of Edinburgh Golfers. He began testing his invention in 1891, but it was only in 1894 after the club was given the 'thumbs up' by the local professional golfers that he placed it on the open market.

Golf (magazine) 26 January 1894 ran a detailed report on the new Urquhart mechanical club:

The blade of the club is moveable. It is fixed by means of a spring into the iron socket at the end of the wooden shaft, this socket being a kind of cogwheel arrangement, which hinders the head from moving or becoming loose. The face of the club could be turned to any angle of loft so that off the tee the blade would be straight…by pressing a small button at the socket the spring holding the blade is released, and by turning the blade back one or two niches in the cog-wheel arrangement and the button released, the club is ready for an iron shot.

An early Urquhart patent adjustable iron *circa* 1895.

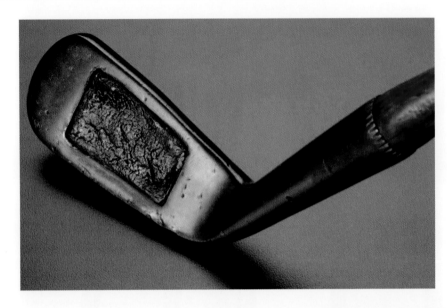

LEFT: A leather-faced Nicoll iron stamped W. & G. Braid, Baltimore CC, *circa* 1898.

BELOW: Socket-headed woods came into fashion at the turn of the twentieth century. Seen here are the two distinct designs. The top club has its shaft only partially inserted into the head and is called a 'blind bore'. The other club has the shaft pushed right through the head and is known as a 'through bore'.

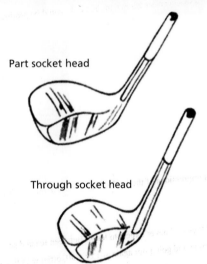

Part socket head

Through socket head

The object of his mechanical adjustable iron was to make a single club take the place of a whole set, or at least to reduce the number of irons that needed to be carried in the golf bag. It was easy to convert to left-handed or right-handed for that tricky shot when up against an obstruction that could restrict the normal path of a swing, for example, the wall at the St Andrew's 17th Road Hole. For the less competitive golfer, what a great companion when walking the dog to have one club capable of hitting shots anywhere between 100 and 200 yards!

A quick and simple modification could turn the Urquhart club into a lofter or even a putter. Adjustable clubs enjoyed a resurgence in the 1920s, and were even made as recently as the 1950s, until eventually they were deemed illegal to use by the R & A.

The **George Nicoll leather-faced cleek**, No.15,425 (1893), had a much shorter and thicker blade than other cleeks, and a shortish hosel. The face of the blade had a 1 x 2in (2.5 x 5cm) cavity to hold a leather insert held in place by glue. The idea behind the patent was that the leather – and later gutta-percha – gave the ball more grip than non-faced irons. The cleek was also advertised as being a useful putter. Spalding later brought out its own cleek, branded as the 'Spalding Cran'. Often the insert leather shrank, creating an uneven striking face, and eventually fell out. Consequently, a club of this type with an intact face insert can fetch a premium at auction.

Francis Archibald Fairlie patented the first of the so-called **'anti-shank' iron clubs** (No.6,681) in 1891. In 1894, the second of these 'anti-shank' clubs was marketed as the **'G.F. Smith Patent'**. The idea behind the club was to produce an iron with no neck area between the blade and hosel (a mis-struck shot can come off the shank or neck of the hosel). Smith's hosel was bent in gooseneck fashion so the blade edge was lined up under the shaft.

Francis Wentworth Brewster's simplex crosshead was made under patent No.9,514 in 1897. Brewster

A Francis Brewster simplex crosshead centre-shafted play club, *circa* 1897.

The aluminium version of the Nicola putter is harder to find than the ones in brass.

COLLECTORS' DOS & DON'TS

Aluminium-headed clubs really clean up well, and the ones fitted with decorative wooden block inserts make a great display. However, the one area of weakness with these clubs is at the top of the neck hosel where the shaft joins the head – look out for cracks to the aluminium, where they have oxidized. Such clubs are worthless today. Also, because aluminium is such a soft material, the heads tend to become quite dented, and this can detract from the value of a club.

The gaps between the teeth on this rake iron were supposed to make it easier to hit the ball out of water!

Left: A large mammoth Niblick measuring 4¹/₂ x 3³/₃in (11 x 9.5cm).
Centre: A George Nicoll leather-faced cleek circa 1892.
Right: An early Urquhart patent adjustable iron circa 1895.

described the shape of the club head as being 'boat-like', which not only referred to the outline of the head, but also the sole of the club. Brewster wanted to replace iron-headed clubs with a set of six simplex crosshead clubs, ranging from a driver as shown here, a long spoon, mid spoon and short spoon through to a pitcher and a putter. In 1902 Brewster added a further two types of club to the set. Brewster's simplex clubs are considered prize collectables.

There were, of course, many more strange and wonderful-looking clubs, too many to cover here – but look out for Spalding's spring-faced iron *circa* 1905, and the James R. Brown rake iron, *circa* 1905–1910, with six upward-facing teeth and attractive decorative scroll-work to its face, used to extract the ball from watery lies and from out of bunkers. Of course it must have been a great conversation piece while standing on the first tee, and in all likelihood was probably more of a novelty than a serious implement.

PATENTED PUTTERS

Willie Park's patented bent-neck putter, No.20,914 in 1894, remains a popular addition to all good club collections. The original model manufactured by Park can be distinguished by its markings in capitals, 'PARK'S SPECIAL' in a circle, with 'PATENT' in a straight line across the back. The salient principle of the club was to keep the hands in front of the ball. What has changed today? There are plenty of copies of this putter that claim to be the 'original bent-neck putter'; however, the

This general golfing advertisement dates back to 1902.

lofted face used for chipping. Sounds too good to be true, and the golfing authorities quickly outlawed it, hence the reason why so few were made.

Captain G. H. Harrison of the Royal Isle of Wight Golf Club designed and invented a **croquet-style putter** in the early 1900s that was made from brass metal. The traditional method of putting can lead to the head of the putter being easily swung off line, leading to all kinds of missed puts. Harrison's novel invention allowed for a simplification of the stroke by the golfer straddling both feet either side of the line of put 'croquet style', then swinging the putter like a pendulum along the line. Therefore the face of the putter and the path of the putter head would be kept square to the hole, so eliminating the possibility of missing so many short puts. Both sides of the blade could be used, and its rounded ends ensured that no accidental damage was caused to the golfer's body.

The unusual shaft is made from a single piece of light-coloured wood, and its handle has eight facets or sides that taper neatly into a round shaft at the bottom, which fits into the club's hosel. In 1899 *Golf Illustrated* reviewed the club and commented on the handle that 'sentiment and tradition apart, this strikes us as giving a surer grip of the club than the ordinary circular leather-covered handle…'

Metal and Aluminium Clubs and Putters

It is often a surprise to golfers to learn that metal woods were first launched at the end of the nineteenth century; many think that 'metal heads' were a new invention in the late 1970s! The first patent for a metal wood was issued to William Currie in 1891, although the material he used was a brass head with a protruding face made from gutta-percha, the same material as used to make the golf ball at that time. In early 1894 both Malcolm Drummond and Thomas V. Vesey received patents for similar-looking woods made from aluminium and steel, both with a gutta-percha face insert.

While both Ralph Neville in 1893 and Thomas Yeomans in 1894 specified aluminium in their patents for a metal wood club, it was the third person to receive a patent, Reginald T. D. Brougham patented as

original putters do not have 'original' stamped on the back of the head.

William Nicol's 'Nicola' duplex, or double-faced putter/club, patented as No.13,307 in 1904, is a very rare putter today. There was a choice of metals used to make the club: aluminium or brass. Of the handful that has come to auction in the last twenty years, the aluminium-headed club is rarer than the brass-headed version – though both types are very rare indeed and valuable. How did the Nicola club work? By using one end of the club in the manner of a snooker cue, the sight lines to the incurved faces (rhomboid in shape) enabled the golfer to use the sole of the club as a striking surface 'allowing short putts to be holed with ease and accuracy'. At the other end was a deeply scored

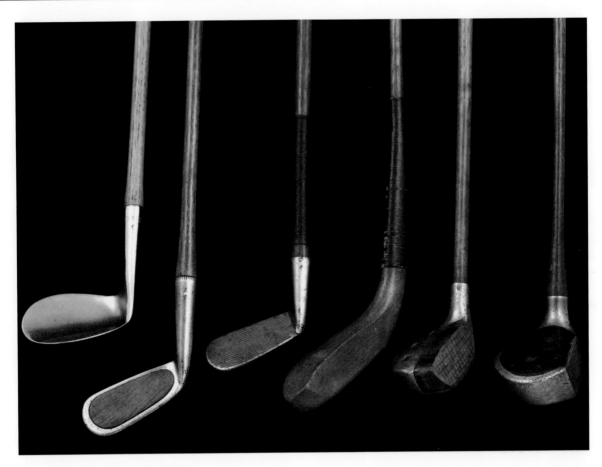

No. 2,416 in 1894, whose aluminium club was the first to be produced in any significant numbers. Conceptually he wanted a club that was more durable and weather-resistant than those made from wood. The resulting club was a bulger-shaped driver with a facial cavity into which a wood block was inserted. The wood

COLLECTORS' DOS & DON'TS

There are fakes on the market, so be careful with your money. Some fraudsters have perfected converting what were snooker/billiard cues into what appear to be genuine Sunday clubs. Snooker cues are, of course, made from ash, whereas golf shafts were of hickory. Even so, not easy to distinguish to the untrained eye!

was secured with a screw through the sole. With hard gutty balls tearing up the faces of most wooden clubs, one of his selling points was the quick replacement of the face without losing the investment of the whole club. Brougham's clubs are marked with an ace of clubs and the motto 'Clubs are Trumps'.

In 1899, Willie Dunn Jr, who had become professional to a golf club in New York, USA, invented and advertised for sale his short hosel 'Indestructible Combination Wood' comprising two different materials, aluminium and wood. The head of the club was made from an aluminium casing, replacing both the lead at the back and the normal metal sole plate found on most woods. Into the open central crown of the head was inserted a snugly fitting block of seasoned wood, which extended through to the face and gave a very solid feel as the grain of the wood ran directly with the strike from front to back. This very durable head had no back lead weight, horn insert or sole plate to come loose, and if

Left to right: A Walter Hagen concave sand iron circa 1928; a Spalding cran iron with wooden face insert; a Spalding gold medal, spring face cleek circa 1902; a Peter McEwan driver circa 1860s; a Willie Park indestructible combination wood, circa 1900; and another part wood, part metal club, maker unknown.

ever damaged, the central wood piece could be easily replaced once the five sole screws were removed.

Meanwhile back in the UK, Sir William Mills had founded the Standard Golf Company in the 1890s. Its factory was situated at the Atlas works in Bonners Field, Sunderland, in the north-east of England. Mills was also to become famous as being the inventor of the Mills hand grenade, used extensively during World War II.

Mills was convinced that wood changed its characteristics when wet, to the detriment of good golf shots. He began by copying the shape of a long-nose wooden putter, and casting it in an aluminium alloy – and in 1900 he introduced his K (Kirkaldy) model long nose putter. The L (low) model soon followed. Both were instant successes, and Mills began making other mallet head models to reflect the variations in length, width and facial depth of other old wooden putters. The X range was named after Harold Hilton; the Y range after James Braid. Mills' range comprised more than twenty putter models between 1900 and 1930. Aluminium woods were introduced, and they were extremely popular in the early 1900s. Consequently, at their height the Mills' Standard Golf Co. was able to advertise a range of over forty different models of aluminium putters and fairway clubs.

TRAVIS AND HIS FAMOUS PUTTER

One of the most collectable aluminium-headed putters is the Schenectady – the world's first ever centre-shafted, bore-through putter.

In June 1904, an American golfer called Walter Travis (born in Australia and winner of the 1900, 1901 and 1903 US Amateur) used his Schenectady putter to win the Amateur Championship in Britain. Travis was not only the first American to win the coveted event, but also the first 'foreigner' to do so, and in the process made the Schenectady putter internationally famous. It

THE QE2 SWILKEN GOLF CLUBS

Ever heard of the QE2 Swilken golf clubs? Maybe these clubs were the worst investment in the twentieth century...from the QE2?

When Sandhill (Bullion) Ltd heard that the world's greatest ocean liner, the QE2 was to undergo a major refit between 1986 and 1987, Sandhill purchased the ship's pair of propellers in order to convert them into limited edition sets of golf clubs. Sandhill then approached the well known club manufacturers, Swilken of St Andrews, to form a joint venture to produce 7,500 sets (yes, 7,500 sets!). Each golf club featured the official QE2 logo, and each club was individually numbered. Of the 7,500 sets, 33 per cent were sold to a Japanese promotions company, each set retailing at £6,200 in Japan. Mr Malcolm Ableson, managing director of Sandhil Swilken, said at the time: 'This order is the most valuable single golf equipment export order to Japan ever placed in the UK.'

The set comprised three woods, nine irons, and a hickory-shafted putter along with an array of complimentary extras such as bags, all presented in a wooden crate. A Sandhill Swilken spokesperson said at the time, 'Our QE2 clubs combine the best in history, tradition and craftsmanship, and provide a unique memento of the past as well as an investment for the future.'

Value today: £250.

had been invented a few years before by an American golfer called Bill Knight who lived in the Schenectady district of New York. Travis saw an early model of the putter at his club and was soon in contact with Knight to order one.

When he received it, Travis was understood to have said that it was 'the best putter I have ever used.' Knight's reasoning behind the putter's design was twofold: first, the centre shaft reduced torque or twisting at impact; and second, the shape of the head enabled the player to align himself better on the putting green. Within days of the Travis win in 1904, Spalding, who had bought the production rights

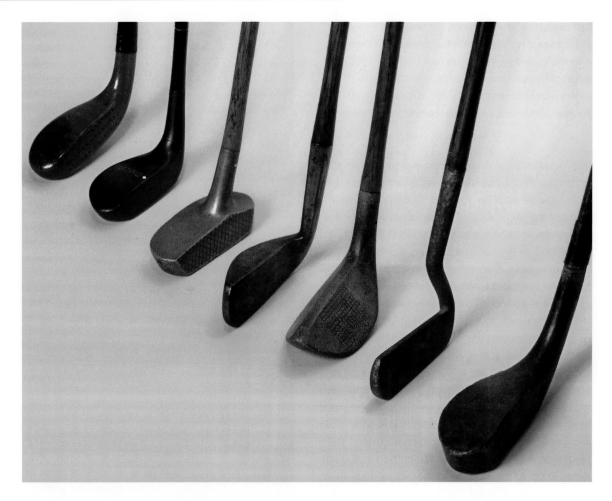

Third from the left: An aluminium putter in the style of a Travis Schenectady putter. The other alloy-headed club is a Duplex, with two identical faces.

from Knight, received orders to make nearly 3,000 Spalding putters stamped 'Spalding American Club Schenectady'. These retailed at 6s 6d each. However, as is often the case between 1904 and 1916, thousands of look-alike Schenectady putters were produced. The most valuable and collectable today must carry the Spalding mark.

This putter created a rift between the game's two golfing bodies, and the R & A declared the putter illegal in 1910. After five years of often heated discussion, the R & A were unhappy with centre-shafted putters that could be easily used croquet-style (not in the true spirit of the game!). The USGA disagreed, stating that putters such as the Schenectady would remain legal in their competitions. They enjoyed plenty of support, not only from the thousands of average golfers who used these putters, but also the US President, William Howard Taft! It was only in 1951 that the R & A finally lifted their ban.

The 1920s and 1930s

This period was known as the 'fancy face' and 'waterfall face' period, when the pace for golf club production and design was being set by American club manufacturers such as Wilson, Spalding, Burke and Kroydon. However, new designs still emanated from the UK. For example, the Dint woods made by Cogswell & Harrison had a face and sole covered by an integral or one-piece 'silver' plate.

The need for lead back weights began to diminish

These matching Spalding Kro-Flite 'Robert T. Jones' irons with wooden shafts are the ultimate collectable for anyone interested in the great man.

with the use of larger club heads, particularly as weight could now be added to the bottom of the club under the sole plate. Woods began to appear with a decorative top or crown, an effect known as 'stripe top'. Decorative faces with coloured ivory inserts such as playing card symbols, Maltese Crosses and other geometric patterns became fashionable in the Art Deco period of the 1920s and 1930s. Soon matching wooden clubs became the norm, as did the numbering of these clubs, with No.1 being the driver. Maybe 'fancy face' woods were a reflection of the decadent times in America? Golf was being portrayed as a fun sport, played by fun people, so why shouldn't the clubs look fun too? Fancy face woods with wooden shafts are very collectable, with America being the most buoyant market.

During the 1920s and 1930s many manufacturers, and especially American ones, also produced irons that had fancy faces – and they were not just pretty, because

they were designed to help the average golfer by imparting spin on the ball (at least, the average golfer thought he needed this extra spin). There were many registered trademarks and face designs. Later these face markings were deemed to be illegal by golf's governing bodies.

Club names included Bakspin, Baxpin, Holdem, Hold-em, Dedli, Deadun, Jerko and Stopum. Face types comprised corrugated or ribbed lines and included designs known as brickwork, tyre tread, slotted with grooves, waterfall, double waterfall, rainbox, dimple-faced, bricks and grooves and waffle.

Prominent manufacturers were Spalding, McGregor, Burke, Wilson, Nicoll, Wm Gibson, Kroydon, Wright & Ditson and Ben Sayers, to name a few only.

In 1929, the R & A legalized steel shafts in Britain. Some club manufacturers disguised the steel shaft with a Pyratone covering to make them look like wooden shafts, or at least 'hoodwink' the old school of golfers into thinking that they were wooden-shafted clubs. These have only limited appeal today, and are cheap to buy.

Classic Clubs from the 1950s to 1990

From the 1940s onwards, American manufacturers dominated the golf club market with their mass production technology: the day of the small club-making firm was soon to reach its end. A policy of advertising heavily, together with endorsement from the game's top players, quickly brought riches to those companies. Amongst the big names were Spalding, Wilson, and in particular, MacGregor.

The latter started in the early 1890s with the help of Scottish club maker Robert White. MacGregor produced wonderfully shaped clubs, both woods and irons, during their golden years from 1940 through to the start of the metal wood period in the late 1970s. The shape and quality of their 'toe grain' persimmon head woods were desired by most of the game's top players, which in turn created a 'must have' for millions of amateur golfers worldwide. At their height in the 1960s and 1970s, MacGregor 'key hole' woods commanded a high price – some tour professionals would pay hundreds of pounds to secure a driver they felt they could use to play better golf. Professionals at this time were *shapers* of the ball, unlike the power player of today, so how the club looked, how it sat, how deep the face was, and how much loft it had, were vital ingredients in the hands of the skilled player. Most often MacGregor and Slazenger woods provided answers to these questions simply by looking so good, and being constructed with the best oil-hardened, tight-grained persimmon wood.

Progress is inevitable, and with it came the introduction of the first hollow head, all-metal wood in the late 1970s. Northwestern Golf Company in the USA were among the very first to bring out this type of head – but Taylor Made developed the market further, calling their metal wood 'Pitsburg persimmon'. There was quite a resistance to the all-metal head by a great many golfers initially, especially amongst tour pros. It was more difficult for the expert player to shape the ball to produce draw and fade with the hollow, or be it foam-filled metal head – but for high handicappers it was great. First, they did not have to bother about looking after their woods, as wet weather, loose sole plates, loose or cracked inserts and in particular skied shots that would mark the varnish finish on a wooden head club, did not affect this material; and they also had a club that helped them to hit the ball straighter!

Manufacturers loved the metal head because it was much cheaper and easier to produce than the 'hands on' creating of a wooden head golf club, with all its processes of neck drilling, inserting, head shaping, sanding, staining and varnishing. So less skill was needed in the factory. The metal head was produced for them by a casting company, and once a mould was made, thousands of identical heads could be produced very easily. Manufacturers began to expect their heavily endorsed tour professionals to show the way and to start playing with them in tournaments, which they did.

At around the same time the graphite shaft was making its appearance. Lighter than steel, it encouraged more club head speed and therefore more distance. It was also much easier to fit into the short neck or hosel of a metal wood than the infinitely more difficult long neck of a wooden club. So within five years, wood head production had ceased, the classic club was no longer used, and the new era with its new materials had replaced the old.

Because of mass production, hardly any club after the end of the hickory period in the late 1920s is regarded as collectable. There are a few exceptions, such as the early Ping putters that were stamped by Slazenger of Wakefield, England, with the names of Jack Nicklaus and Gary Player, both players being contracted to play with Slazenger clubs in the 1970s.

As the new Ping putters were not selling very well, Slazenger – the first company to sell them in the UK – decided to stamp them with the names of their two stars in order to promote sales. However, it seems that the two players were not being paid to endorse them, and when they found out, they asked for their names to be removed. Therefore only a small number were stamped, and it is these that have become collectable. But in recent years their values have fallen from around £500 to £200. Why? Because a new generation of Scotty Cameron (Tiger Woods putts with one) collectors have replaced the older generation of Ping putter enthusiasts!

Nowadays very few modern woods or irons are ever

The Holtzapetal-type golf exercise walking stick with the leather cover was sold in the Gamages Gardening Department in 1900 as a weedcutter.

referred to as being 'collectable', simply because so many clubs have been produced. The only remaining area of desirability seems to be in the model of putter that has been, or is being, used by the stars of the professional tour. Golfers will want one in the hope that it will improve their own golf. Well, hasn't that been the story all down the ages!

Sunday Walking Sticks and Clubs

An interesting and popular golfing theme is that of collecting walking sticks fashioned in the shape or form of golf clubs. These were often made in the winter when the club makers had relatively little to do as a means of supplementing their income, or even as apprentice pieces.

Even as recently as the 1890s, British citizens were expected to 'behave civilly and Christianly...' on the Sabbath. Certainly in Scotland it was forbidden to play any sports, including golf, on Sundays. However, while walking the dog on the links, there was nothing wrong in having a swing or two, before casting a furtive look to see that all was clear and having a swish at a ball with an upturned 'walking stick'!

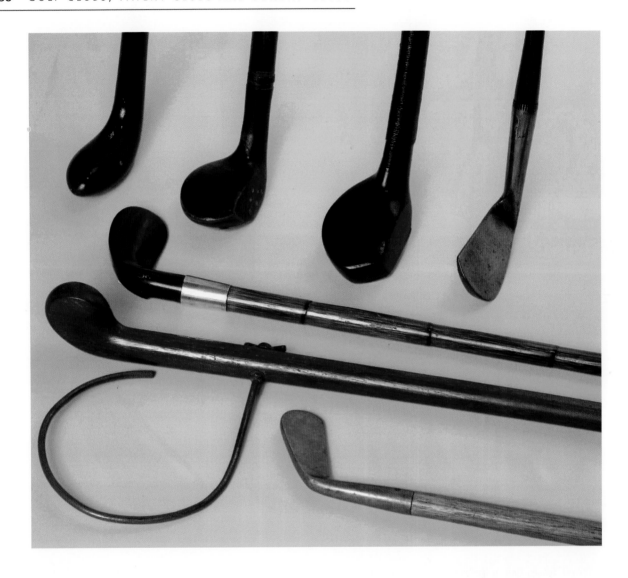

A fine selection of Sunday walking sticks to choose from.

Extracts from the registers of South Leith Parish on 12 March 1724 read as follows:

John Groser compeared and declared that he and William Barclay, servant to Alexander Bruno Shambo, Breech Maker in Edinburgh, on the Sabbath last saw three Gentlemen come out to the Links, two of them carrying Clubs under their coats, and saw them lay down their Golf Balls and fall to the playing and play for some time at the east end of the Links. The Session

having heard and considered this affair Think it proper that a narration of the above matter may by the R. R. Ministers be laid before the Right Hon. The Lord Justice Clerk in order to the punishing and preventing such bare faced profanation of the Lord's day…

It soon became common for a golfer's walking stick to be fashioned after real golf clubs – in fact, at first glance they resemble small-headed golf clubs. The main difference is that a walking stick's wooden 'shaft' has a reverse taper, in that it comes to a point at the grip end.

There are many styles of Sunday club, with heads being made to simulate tortoiseshell, some with a bone

sole insert, and some fitted with an integral triangular face insert and sole plate. Some would feature a silver-plated, engraved collar to take an inscription. In 1912, J. Ferguson made Sunday clubs with an integral mahogany snuff-box handle holding a silver snuff box lined with mother-of-pearl. Another very collectable example is the golf ball walking cane *circa* 1930, with

And more Sunday walking sticks to look at.

silver band, brass handle designed as a mesh-patterned golf ball, and an ebonized shaft.

Other well known makers included D. Anderson & Son and James Mayo of Walton on Thames.

The golfer's library, for endless hours of reading and research.

THE LITERATURE
OF GOLF

In 1970 an American collector was doing some research in the St Andrews public library. One of the assistants was going around the library with a trolley, and began to throw golf books from the shelves on to the floor. He couldn't believe it, as these books were old and fragile.

'Stop!' he cried, 'What are you doing?' She told him that later that week the library was receiving a consignment of newer books, and she had been told to make space by throwing these older ones out. The collector quickly checked the books lying on the floor, and asked

BOOK TERMINOLOGY

SOME POPULAR BOOK SIZES

Crown: A popular traditional paper size measuring about 7½ x 5in (19 x 13cm).

Octavo: Usually written simply '8vo', it indicates a book of between about 7 and 10in (18 and 25cm) in height. Larger than A4 and smaller than A3.

Quarto: Usually written '4to', it describes a book of a distinctly large, square shape, about the size and shape of a standard telephone directory.

Royal: A larger paper size, measuring 25 x 20in (213 x 200cm).

SOME POPULAR BOOK TERMS

a.e.g.: All the page edges are gilded.

Bookplate: Also known as an 'ex libris' – an ownership label, often decorative, that is usually pasted to the front endpaper: this is known as 'pastedown'.

Calf: The most common bookbinding leather, smooth textured and capable of taking most dyes.

Cloth: Widely used as a covering material since about 1830: original cloth is that commissioned by the publisher, whereas binder's cloth is a rebinding.

Endpaper: The paper lining to the inside binding: the paste-down is pasted to the cover, and the free endpaper protects the text block.

f.e.p.: The front endpaper; f.f.e.p. is sometimes used for the 'front free endpaper'.

Foxing: Reddish-brown (fox-coloured) spotting.

Frontispiece: Or simply 'frontis', the plate facing the title page.

Prelims: Preliminaries, or preliminary leaves: all the pages – title page, contents, preface, list of illustrations – preceding the main body of the text.

t.e.g.: The top edge of the page is gilded.

Verso: The reverse of a leaf.

Wrapper: Usually a soft material to make the book's cover.

SOME COMMON CONDITION RATINGS

Mint (m): Absolutely as new.

Fine (f): Excellent.

Near fine (nf): Almost as good as fine.

Very good (vg): Much better than average.

Good (g): A perfectly acceptable second-hand copy, but with evidence of age and use.

Fair: More than average wear and tear.

Working copy: Poor, but usable and complete.

Reading copy: Capable of being read, but little more.

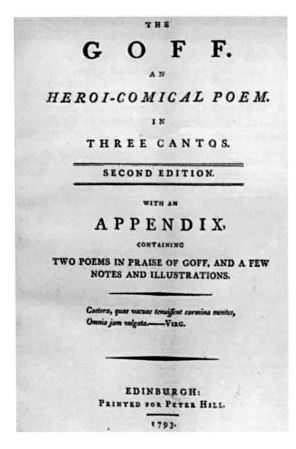

THE

G O F F.

AN

HEROI-COMICAL POEM.

IN

THREE CANTOS.

SECOND EDITION.

WITH AN

APPENDIX,

CONTAINING

TWO POEMS IN PRAISE OF GOFF, AND A FEW
NOTES AND ILLUSTRATIONS.

Coetera, quae vacuas tenuiffent carmina mentes,
*Omnia jam vulgata.——*VIRG.

EDINBURGH:
PRINTED FOR PETER HILL.

1793.

Probably the most expensive golf book ever, with prices starting at £20,000.

This collection of *The Golfing Annual* needs only a few more to be complete…what a source of information. These annuals are to golfers what Wisden's Almanac is to cricketers.

if he could buy them, rather than let them be thrown out. He was asked to make a donation to the library, so he wrote a cheque for £100, a reasonably hefty sum of money then, and the library posted him the collection of books at no further charge. Amongst them was a good copy of Webster Glynes' *The Maiden: A Golfing Epic*, published in 1893 – and in 1970 it was valued at $18,000! So our American collector was certainly in the right place at the right time!

Long gone are the days when you could drop into a dusty old back-street shop and find a copy of a late nineteenth-century golf book languishing under a layer of dust at a knock-down price – though maybe today there are still bargains to be had on the various Internet auction sites. It has been estimated that there have been well over 10,000 golf books published, in various languages, since the first book to be devoted entirely to

golf, Thomas Mathison's *The Goff*, first published in 1743 – so there is plenty to choose from.

The literature of golf embraces the history of the game, and anyone wanting to start a golf library may wish to specialize in one of the following genres: annuals, course design and maintenance, autobiographies and biographies, catalogues, club histories and handbooks, and so on, as discussed in more detail below.

Annuals

Golf annuals and year books are valuable sources of information. *The Golfing Annual* was first published in 1888: initially C. Robertson Bauchope was the editor, but in 1889 David Scott Duncan took over. The run of annuals ended with the twenty-third edition in 1910. These are generally agreed to be the most important record of golf at the end of the nineteenth century and early part of the twentieth century, covering the transition from the gutta-percha ball era to that of the rubber-cored ball, with information on golf clubs, players, results, layout plans of golf courses, charts and photographs, as well as trade advertisements.

ABOVE: *The Golfer's Handbook* is a wonderful source of golf information. Beldam was an early twentieth-century photographer well ahead of his time.
RIGHT: Did *The Irish Golfer's Annual* only get to the 'advance proof' stage in 1897?

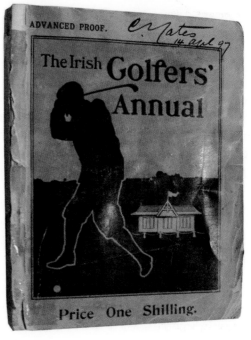

Another superb reference is *Golf: The Badminton Library*: although not strictly an annual, several editions of the same book have appeared over the years. First published in 1890, there were initially four 1890 editions: the first trade large page edition (250 copies); the first American edition (also the first book on golf ever published in America); and two revised editions. Altogether there were eight editions, with the ninth being published in 1911. The first (1890) and seventh (1901) editions remain the hardest to come by.

The Golfer's Handbook was first published in 1899, and has been produced continually since then, except for the war years 1942 to 1946.

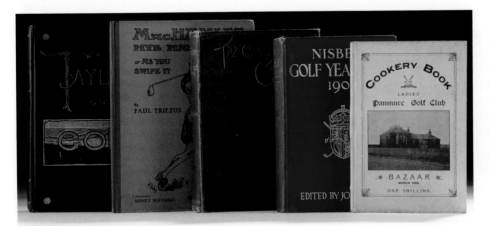

Willie Park's *The Game of Golf* was the first golf book to be written by a golf professional. The Panmure Golf Club's cookery book was published to raise monies for the club.

Architectural, Course Design and Maintenance

There were several books published over the last century on golf courses and golf course design and construction, which because of their 'readability' continue to command high prices when sold. Some examples to look for include the following:

Horace Hutchinson's *British Golf Links: A Short Account of the Leading Golf Links of the United Kingdom*, published in 1897. As golf exploded on to the sporting scene worldwide, noted amateur golfer and acclaimed writer Horace Hutchinson chronicled the great British courses at the turn of the twentieth century, and successfully profiled more than fifty courses within the book's 331 pages.

Many of the courses are golf's most legendary venues. Each chapter contains extensive historical information utilizing historical accounts and information provided by the various club secretaries to include hole-by-hole descriptions, yardages and general hints on playing them.

In 1906 the same author also wrote *Golf Greens and Green Keeping*, and this is regarded as being an important book on the proper maintenance of the course, including soil management, grass cutting and preparation of hazards.

H. N. Wethered and T. Simpson's *Architectural Side of Golf* has long been seen as a masterpiece on golf architecture, being a most thorough analysis of the strategic school of design. It was published in 1929,

and comprises 210 pages, with forty-four plates and twenty-six etchings.

Another sought-after book on the subject is *Golf Architecture in America: Its Strategy and Construction*, written by George C. Thomas in 1927, and consisting of 342 pages and sixty-six plates. Thomas was a renowned Californian golf architect, best known for designing the Riviera Country Club in Los Angeles. This book is now regarded as being one of the premier works on the genre and one of the most famous early American works on golf course design…a 'must-have' book.

Another gem that is small in size but big in information, is Alister J. MacKenzie's *Golf Architecture: Economy in Course Construction and Green Keeping* as published in 1920; and a similar era classic is Robert Hunter's *The Links*, released in 1926. This is one of the earliest American publications on golf architecture, and features several American golf courses.

Autobiographies and Biographies

These range from early autobiographical books written by professionals from the turn of the twentieth century such as Sandy Herd and Harry Vardon, and later by Henry Cotton and Walter Hagen, to biographies on famous golfers such as Bobby Jones. These remain popular and can still be found at a reasonable price, although they may not be first editions.

An example of a biography is W. W. Tulloch's definitive book on Tom Morris published in 1908. It has a rather long and cumbersome title – *The Life of Tom*

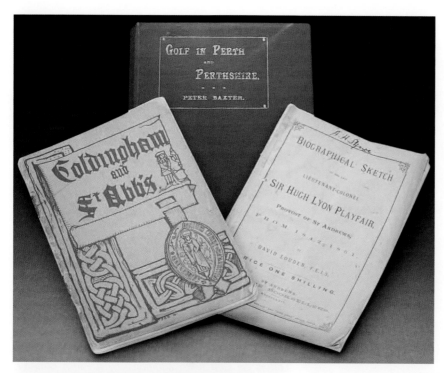

LEFT: Three scarce titles. Sir Hugh Lyon Playfair's book gives a fascinating insight into how golf started and evolved in India during the mid to late 1800s.

BELOW: Those were the days, when a golf club cost £2 and a golf ball 1s 6d!

Morris, with Glimpses of St. Andrews and its Golfing Celebrities – but it is a classic golfing book, the corner stone of any library, and remains to this day essential reading for the golfing enthusiast. It has 334 pages, with twenty-seven illustrations scattered throughout. In the book, Tulloch charts the fascinating life of this humble club carrier, feather ball maker, custodian of the links (green keeper) and Open champion golfer on four occasions, who went on to become the Royal & Ancient Club's green keeper, the last four years being an honorary appointment until his death in 1908. His funeral was an occasion for national and international mourning, as Old Tom Morris was synonymous with St Andrews and with golf. In 1982 Tulloch's book was reprinted as a facsimile edition, 200 copies being bound in leather.

Catalogues

This section includes auction house catalogues and golf manufacturer trade catalogues. The former go back to the early 1980s, when Sotheby's and Christie's led the way with their golf sales, initially held in Scotland. These publications offer an incredible amount of information,

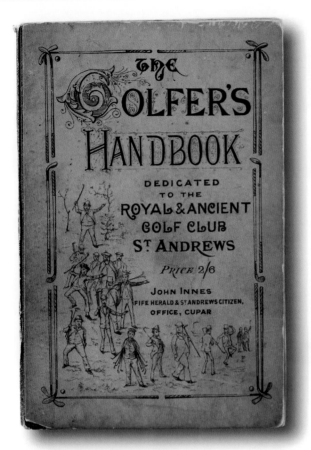

This pre-first edition of *The Golfer's Handbook* sold at auction in 2007 for over £7,000.

and usually cover every aspect of the hobby. The realized prices are important, too.

Trade catalogues date back to the end of the nineteenth century. An example is the Iver Johnson Sporting Goods (Boston) catalogue published in 1899–1900. Inside there is an outstanding black and white picture of the first moulded mesh Haskell golf ball, plus a listing of twenty-three gutty balls, such as the Henley and the Musselburgh.

Classic and Rare

These are books where there are few budget restraints, or none at all. If 'rare' and 'expensive' are the two predominant factors to be considered, then here are five such books (of course this is a subjective list and there are many others):

Rules of the Thistle Golf Club; with Some Historical Notices Relative to the Progress of the Game of Golf in Scotland. Published in 1824, this is the first book devoted in its entirety to golf. It comprises fifty-six pages, of which eleven are devoted to a set of rules 'drawn up for regulating the concerns of their fraternity'.

Another classic would be Robert Forgan's *The Golfer's Handbook*, a first edition (advance copy) from 1881, comprising seventy-eight pages of instruction, history, golfing feats and so on. The book went into numerous reprintings, and by 1897 its title had changed to *The Golfers' Manual*.

One of the most important books in early golf, and the first anthology, is George Robb's *Historical Gossip about Golf and Golfers*, fifty-eight pages and published in 1863.

Another classic, rare and expensive book with only sixty-eight pages is James Balfour's *Reminiscences of Golf on St Andrews Links*, published in 1887.

And last, but not least, is the Reverend Lawson's *Letters on Golf (with additions) by a Parish Minister*, comprising only sixty-four pages and published in 1889. There are fewer than five surviving copies of this thin missive. In the book the 'Prefatory Note' explains: 'These letters, reprinted with a few corrections and additions from the *Elgin Courant & Courier*, had their origin in a desire to make better known the game of golf in the Laigh of Moray in view of the recently formed Moray Golf Club…'

Club Histories and Club Handbooks

With so many golf clubs now being 100 or more years old, there are numerous centenary books to collect and read. They are usually very informative, and more often than not relatively inexpensive. W. E. Hughes' *Chronicles of Blackheath Golfers with Illustrations and Portraits*, published in 1897, is the first published history of any club, and comprises fascinating portraits of members and their playing records. Club handbooks, especially those published in the 1920s and 1930s, are very collectable – look out for the ones by Bernard Darwin, as these always sell with a premium. In recent years both types of book in this category have proved

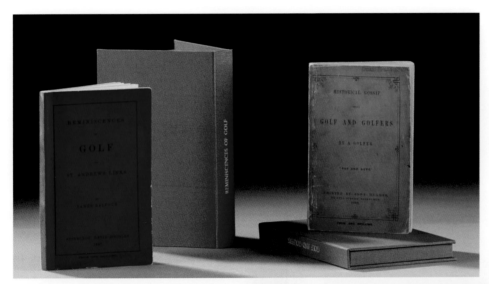

These two rare and fragile books are kept safe in personalized clam shell boxes.

These booklets extolling the virtues of the Pinehurst golf resort at the beginning of the twentieth century are keenly sought after today.

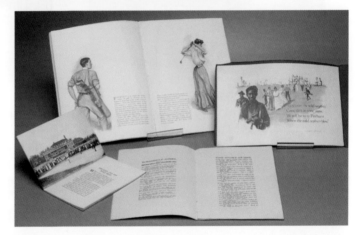

useful references for the lake divers who search for sunken golf balls. The old plans often show redundant ponds and ditches long since drained or filled in.

First Editions

These tend to be the rarest and most valuable copies. Often the earliest print runs were low in number because the publisher didn't know immediately if they would be a success, so surviving copies are particularly rare and potentially valuable. 'First published' and 'First printed' are the key words, and are usually to be found on the copyright page. Their cachet among collectors means this is the edition they always want, so expect to pay a premium.

Golf Memorabilia

During the first half of the twentieth century there were only a handful of books that touched on golf memorabilia, old equipment, bygone implements and suchlike. Such books would include Simpson's *Art of Golf* (1887) that focused on the historical perspective of the game rather than being aimed at collectors.

The first documented collector of golf memorabilia was Harry B. Wood. During the 1880s and early 1900s, he sought golfing relics north of the border. He had a small but active team of lookers and scouts who would source material for him. He even befriended Old Tom Morris, who sold him clubs and balls. In 1910, Wood published the first dedicated book on golf antiques:

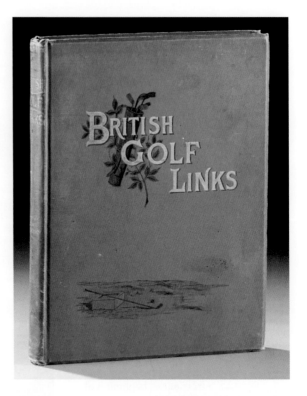

Harry B. Wood was the first true golfing memorabilia collector, and his book is still a great reference.

Horace Hutchinson's *British Golf Links*, first published in 1897, was reprinted some 100 years later. It is a big book at 16in (40cm) high.

Kerr's *The Golfing Book of East Lothian* is a 'must-have' book; Lang's *Golfing Papers* is a fun read; while Clarke's *Golf, A Royal & Ancient Game* is also essential reading.

COLLECTORS' HELPFUL HINTS

BOOKS

- With all books get the best condition you can afford. A well thumbed book can be 10 per cent of a top-notch book.

- An original dust jacket can increase the value by ten-fold.

- If you have a book in pieces it is better to buy a clam box to contain it all, than it is to rebind it.

- Always check for 'extras' that often find their way into the pages of a book, such as letters, invoices, photographs and newspaper cuttings.

- Look for signatures. The price of a book can soar if the author has included a personal message in the book – but beware of fraudsters.

- Enjoy the read, as that is the book's raison d'être. As with most investments, values can go up as well as down. You can not put a price on knowledge gained, or the rewards of a pleasurable read.

- When displaying your books, do not squeeze them tightly on a shelf, as they like to breathe. If not on display, do not store them in damp, cold areas because the pages will buckle, and once damp, it will lead to fox stains caused by mould disease.

- Remember, within the European Union there is no VAT (sales tax) payable on books.

- Limited editions are best signed by the author; however, to have a book personally dedicated may not always add to its value.

- Do check that all pages, plates and maps, and course plans are intact, that there are no graffiti inside, and that the bindings are good.

- Be selective when buying instructional books.

- If you want to get rid of an old price written in pencil on the front flyleaf, or annotated notes inside the book, use a pencil rubber and work from the spine out towards the edges – use short strokes, always in the same direction, and take care not to put too much pressure on the paper. Be especially careful when you are dealing with soft paper, as it will come up very easily.

- Finally, buy a copy of *The Game of Golf and the Printed Word 1566–2005* by Richard E. Donovan and Rand Jerris.

MAGAZINES

- A complete run of magazines is the ideal, but individual magazines that are pre-1940 will be valuable.

- Non-golf magazines featuring golfers on their covers, such as *Life*, can be sought after.

- Check that the contents are clean, that photographs haven't been cut out, and that the covers are intact.

- Buy *Golf International* magazine as it contains a regular two-page feature on golf antiques, readers' letters on memorabilia, and auction reports.

Golfing Curios and the Like. Of course, there have been many books published in the last thirty years devoted to the hobby of collecting golfing artefacts, this book being just one of many!

John and Morton Olman's *The Encyclopaedia of Golf Collectibles: A Collector's Identification and Value Guide*, first published in 1985, 306 pages long, is still regarded as being the 'Bible', and the first book that one still turns to as a quick reference. It is so good that it is as relevant in 2008 as it was in 1985.

History

This remains a most popular category, and there are many titles to find. One is Everard's *A History of the Royal and Ancient Golf Club, St. Andrews, from 1754–1900*, published in 1907. This was the first written and published history of golf played at the St Andrews Golf Club.

Another is Harold H. Hilton and Garden C. Smith's *The Royal & Ancient Game of Golf* published in 1912 in two limited editions of 100 and 900 copies respective-

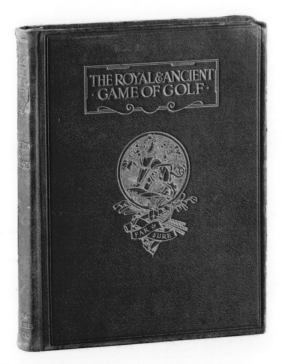

Harold H. Hilton and Garden G. Smith's *The Royal & Ancient Game of Golf*. The red leather edition was limited to 900 copies, whilst the vellum edition was even more special, at just 100 copies.

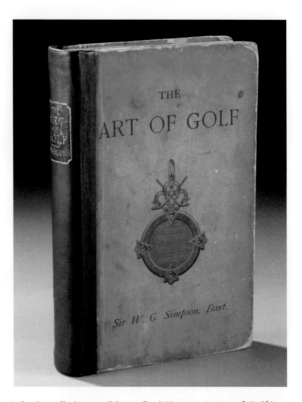

It is virtually impossible to find Simpson's *Art of Golf* in mint condition.

ly. It measures 12 x 9½in (30 x 24cm) and has 275 pages. This really is the ultimate book on golfing history, with twelve detailed chapters and two appendices that cover all aspects of the game. Chapter headings include 'The Game in America', 'Continental Golf', 'Golf, its Origins and History' and 'Theoretical and Practical'. The book is filled with many black and white plates, as well as two fine photogravures and three coloured plates. It just oozes quality. The deluxe edition of 100 books is distinguished by a gilt-lettered, cream vellum hard-backed cover enhanced by a gilt-tooled pictorial lion emblem. In 1986 antiquarian book expert Dick Donovan wrote of this mighty tome, 'This is one of the most magnificent books in the entire library of golf, comprehensive in content, very handsome in appearance, and attractively illustrated.'

A more modern 'must have' historical book would be Ian Henderson and David Stirk's *Golf in the Making*, first published in 1979 and comprising 332 pages. This book set a very high standard, with its thorough research on the origins of golf, clear and precise writing styles, and abundance of never-before-published photographs and drawings. For example, the authors listed over 120 British golf patents on mainly clubs and balls between 1876 and 1914. It is regarded as being the first complete history of the evolution of the game to be published, and it remains a fascinating read and a great reference today.

Humour

Many of us amateurs at golf gain comfort by reading about the golfing tribulations, recorded in word or drawing, of others of similar standard. A good start would be Charles Crombie's *The Rules of Golf Illustrated*, published by Perrier, the mineral water company in 1905. It is a wonderful book that inspired the decoration on Royal Doulton's pottery wares. Others would include the works of P. G. Wodehouse; cartoons of the satirical magazine *Punch*, now long defunct; and

LEFT: *The Irish Golfer* magazine was only published for a short time at the beginning of the twentieth century, and is a rare publication today. ABOVE: These magazines date back to 1891 and are filled with great articles, illustrations and advertisements.

the American cartoons of Clare Briggs. Not to be forgotten would be the much admired cartoonist H. M. Bateman with his *Adventurers at Golf*, first published in 1923 and later reprinted.

Instructional

These are plentiful, but such books do not generally rise much in value, and even the very early instruction books struggle to keep up with books in the other sections. Early and still popular titles include William Park's *The Game of Golf*, first published in 1896 and the first book ever to be written by a professional golfer; George Beldam's *Great Golfers: Their Methods at a Glance* from 1904; and George Beldam and J. H. Taylor's *Golf Faults*

Illustrated, published in 1905. The 1904 publication contained contributions from famous players of the day such as Harry Vardon, Harold H. Hilton, J. H. Taylor, Alex Herd and James Braid.

Magazines and Journals

The contents of the very early magazines, 1890s to 1930s, would often include a diary of golfing events; book reviews; advice to young golfers; letters to the editor; and questions on rules and competition results. All in all they were good reading, and certainly of great research value. They still make for a good read, and the information contained within them is priceless, with editorials on new golfing inventions, and advertisements by club and ball makers, often including graphics of the products.

The first golf magazine was published on 19 September 1890 and was entitled *A Weekly Record of 'Ye Royal and Ancient' Game*. In 1899 its title was changed to *Golf Illustrated*, and that, of course, went on to become one of Britain's most respected and enduring golfing journals.

Other commercial magazine titles to look for would include:

- *Golfing*: first published in 1895.
- *Golfing & Cycling Illustrated*: circa late 1890s.
- *The Irish Golfer - A Weekly Record of the Royal Game*: a very rare publication from the early twentieth century.
- *The American Golfer*: founded in 1908, it was published every other Saturday until October 1925, when it became a monthly. Walter Travis was its first editor; he was later replaced by Grantland Rice.
- *Golfer's Magazine* (Chicago): 1920s onwards.
- *Golfing: The National Golfers' Magazine* (Chicago): first published in 1933; in 1936 its circulation was 300,000.
- *Golfdom: The Business Journal of Golf*: 1930s onwards.

There are also less commercial magazines, ones published as 'in house' literature or as club journals. Examples include:

- *Golfika*: the magazine of the European Association of Golf Historians and Collectors, first published in 2006.
- *Golfiana* Magazine: the international journal for golf historians and collectors, twenty-four issues from spring 1987 to winter 1994. Illustrated from photographs, paintings, drawings, advertisements and so on throughout, showing various golfing scenes, portraits, golf course maps, clubs, balls, equipment, memorabilia. A great shame that it had to cease publishing.
- *The Bulletin* of The Golf Collector's (USA) Society: 1970 to the present day, an important publication,

four per year, preserving the history of the game and promoting the social side, too.
- *Through the Green*, of the British Golf Collectors Society: the 1980s to the present day; an important publication, four per year, preserving the history of the game and promoting the social side, too.
- The *USGA Golf Journal*: the 1950s onwards.

Poetry, Ballads and Songs

This is a small but rewarding section, and it is astounding just how few golf books of poetry and ballads have been published.

The social side of golf has always been important, and is justly recorded in these books and pamphlets. One can imagine early golfers retiring to the smoking room after a superb and lengthy meal following their day at 'goff'. Here their entertainment would be the recitation of poems – some clubs even had their own poet laureate – and the singing of songs and ballads, whilst enjoying a 'wee dram' of the Scottish elixir!

By coincidence, the oldest piece of literature that is devoted entirely to golf is Thomas Mathison's *The Goff. An Heroi-Comical Poem in Three Cantos*. In almost heroic terms, it tells of a match between Pygmalion (the author) and Catalio (Alexander Dunning, a noted Edinburgh golfer of the day). First published in 1743, it comprised twenty-two pages within paper wrappers. This edition named many prominent golfers, and possibly this caused some consternation because in subsequent editions they were only identified by their initials. The second edition was published by James Reid in

BUYER BEWARE

GROUND UNDER REPAIR

A few years ago *Golf Illustrated* magazine gave away an exact sixteen-page facsimile of their 'No.1, Vol 1' magazine. publsished in 1899, with their then current magazine. The paper used was also a giveaway, because it was glossy and had a fake sepia effect.

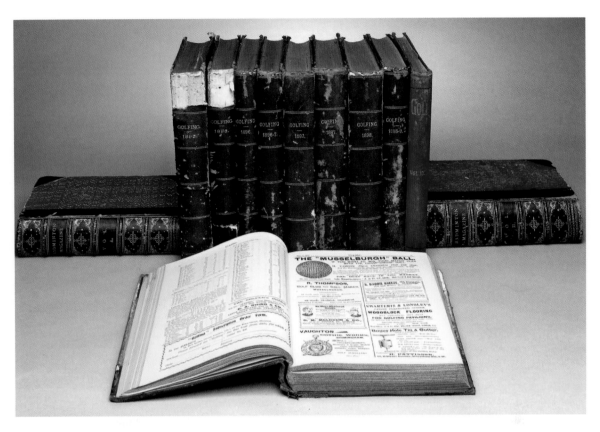

Golf, *Golfing* and *Badminton* magazines: their bindings, although somewhat distressed, could be professionally restored.

1763, and also had twenty-two pages; the third edition, published by Peter Hill in 1793, contained the addition of a dedication that increased the number of pages to thirty-two. Caution should be exercised, however, as this edition is incorrectly identified as the 'second edition'. Some regard the second edition as being the rarest of the three editions, with only five copies existing today in 2008; two are in private collections and three are in institutions. Prices are in excess of £20,000, and are accordingly not for the faint-hearted; many buyers have had to be content with the USGA Museum reprinted edition of 1,400 copies, published in 1981.

Another classic within this section would be Henry Adamson's *The Muses Threnodie: or Mirthful Mournings on the death of Mr. Gall*, as first published in Perth, Scotland, in 1638. This poem, comprising nine 'muses', is the first to make reference to golf in a liter-

ary or book form, and is Adamson's tribute to his late friend and fellow Perth resident, Master Gall:

> 'And yee my Clubs, you must no more prepare
> To make you bals flee whistling in the air.'

There are only six copies known! In the second enlarged edition of 1774, by James Cant, extensive page footnotes give a comprehensive history of Perth from earliest times, as well as an explanatory interpretation of Adamson's writings.

More affordable, and by authors who are easier to read, would be T. Ross Stewart's *Ways of the Links*, first edition 1895, which contains *A Score of Parodies* and is one of the few books dedicated to golf poetry. There are several others that contain perhaps only one or two golfing poems, so unless the rest of the narrative is also about golf (an example being Andrew Lang's *A Batch of Golfing Papers* 1892), it is debatable whether the book warrants inclusion in the 'true literature of golf' category. Nevertheless, some do, and one of these is again a Lang publication: *XXII Balendes in Blue China*, first edition 1886, that contains the *Ballad of the Royal Game of Golf*. Likewise, his *Base and Arniere Urn*, first edition 1894, contained only *Ode to Golf*. It is Lang's St Andrews background, and his prolific output of literature with golf references (including that entitled *St Andrews*), which puts him firmly in the golfing catalogue.

Lang's contemporary, R. F. Murray, is a similar candidate, although to a lesser extent. His *The Scarlet Gown* book of poems, published in varying editions since 1891, contains no more than three on golf. Murray was regarded as the 'poet *par excellence* of St Andrews and its university'. Similarly the Badminton library Poetry of Sport 1896, and the Londsdale library *Anthology of Prose and Verse* 1932, each contains only one or two on golf. Prolific St Andrews author, George Bruce, although a golfer himself, included only two golf-related poems in his *Destiny and Other Poems*, 1876. But it was a classic, for not only was it entitled *In Memory of Young Tom Morris – The Champion Golfer of the World*, but it included a sepia plate of both Old and Young Tom Morris. This book is itself one of the most handsome, and is worthy of a place upon the shelf of any discerning collector.

Other poetry books include:

- Thomas Marsh: *Blackheath Golfing Lays by the Poet-Laureate of the Club*, as printed for the members of the club in 1873. This one will not be easy to find, as only four copies have come to auction in the past twenty years.
- Robert Clark: *Poems on Golf*, published in 1867, a series of poems collected by the members of the Edinburgh Burgess Golfing Society.
- Violet Flint: *A Golfing Idyll* or, *The Skipper's Round with the Deil on the Links of St. Andrews*, published in 1893.
- *Golfiana or a Day at Gullane*, an extremely rare pamphlet of golfing poems dating from 1869.
- J. Thomson: *Golfing and Other Poems and Songs* 1893, a limited edition of just fifty.
- R.K. Risk: *Songs of the Links* published in 1904. The third edition is the rarest of the three.
- George Fullerton Carnegie's poem *Golfiana*, published in 1863.

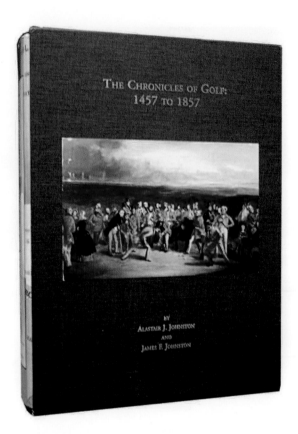

The Chronicles of Golf 1457 to 1857: a 'must-have' book, even though it is quite a heavy read.

- David Jackson (Tailor, Golfer and Poet): *Golf Songs and Recitations*, published in 1895.

When scouring bookshops, it can occasionally be quite rewarding not to neglect the section on poetry, as it may reveal hitherto lesser or unknown golfing poems, secreted within the contents. Such is the case of poetess Sylvia Duff who, in her book *The Flapper's Wish* (1920), has included the moving poem, *The Royal and Ancient Game 1914–1918*.

Recent Classics

Here are my suggested four modern 'must-have' books that would be a cornerstone of any aspiring library, but would also impart almost enough information to keep any golf memorabilia collector satisfied. Their authors were awarded the prestigious Murdoch Medal by the

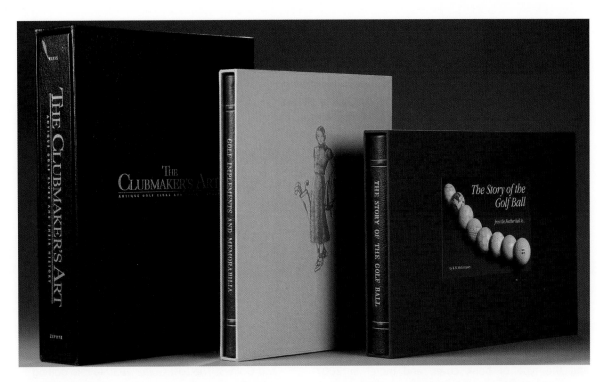

British Golf Collectors Society for their contributions to golf literature.

The Chronicles of Golf 1457 to 1857 has become essential reading for anyone serious about the game or its history and development. It was co-written by Alastair Johnston and his father James F. Johnston in 1993, and with over 700 pages it is not a book for the faint-hearted. As its title implies, it chronicles the development of the game from 1457, the year in which the game of golf is first referred to in a book, up to 1857, the first year of the Grand National Tournament (to become the Open). Only 900 books were published, making it an instant limited edition. The original retail price was £70, and at that time some book reviewers were annoyed that the Johnstons refused to forward 'free' review copies. Nevertheless, it was publicized by word of mouth, and with such a small production run the book sold out very quickly. It has never been reprinted, and this, of course, has enhanced its desirability and value (£800). Each book was numbered by hand and signed by the two authors. Alastair Johnson won the Murdoch Medal in 1994.

The second book is *The Club Maker's Art*, undoubtedly the leading book on golf clubs, written by Jeffery

These are three cornerstone reference books of any modern golf library: let's hope this one is, too!

B. Ellis and published in 1997. A new, double book edition of *The Club Maker's Art* was published in 2007, with additional research and enhanced pictures. Ellis majestically affords his readers detailed specifications of over 300 golf clubs covered by British patents, each one supported by classy photography. Jeff Ellis won the Murdoch Medal in 1998

The Story of the Golf Ball is the definitive book on golf balls from the feathery ball up to small-sized balls made in the early 1970s. Your author Kevin McGimpsey spent over eight years researching and writing the book. Prices realized at auction for golf balls have been included to add further interest. Published in 2003, the book was limited to 1,250 standard books with dust jacket, and 250 in leather and cloth with matching slipcase. Kevin McGimpsey won the Murdoch Medal in 2004.

And finally *The Game of Golf and the Printed Word 1566–1985* was written and compiled by Richard Donovan and Joseph Murdoch. All known golfing books are listed by title in alphabetical order. Each

Bernard Darwin's *Rubs of the Greens* in dust jacket is the ultimate find for a Darwin collector.

book's entry gives details of the author, publisher, the date published, the number of pages and illustrations, and the type of book cover, and more. In 2007 Donovan and Rand Jerris published *The Game of Golf and the Printed Word 1566-2005*, a two volume set, which brought the listing of books and authors up to date. Cloth-bound with a slipcase, the new book contains over 15,000 entries. Dick Donovan (posthumously) and Rand Jerris won the Murdoch Medal in 2007.

Single Author

If you like a particular style of writing, then why not concentrate on your favourite author? Examples could include:

● Bernard Darwin (grandson of Charles): he was called 'the greatest golf writer of all time' by his American counterpart, Herbert Warren Wind. Book titles include: *Golfing Bypaths*; *Green Memories*; *Life is Sweet Brother*; *Second Shots*; *Casual Talks about Golf*; *A Round of Golf on the L.N.E.R.*; *Golf from The Times*; *A History of Golf in Britain*; *Pack Clouds Away*; *Rubs of the Green*; *Playing The Like*; *Golf Between Two Wars*; *The World That Fred Made*; *Every Idle Dream*; *James Braid and Golfing Bypaths*.

● H.G. Hutchinson: *Aspects of Golf*; *The Badminton Library*; *Famous Golf Links*; *The Book of Golf and Golfers*; *The Lost Golfer 1930* (a rare golfing detective novel); *The New Book of Golf*.

● Henry Longhurst: *You Never Know Till You Get There*; *I Wouldn't Have Missed It*; *Spice of Life*; *Golf Mixture*; *The Best of Longhurst*; *Candid Caddies*; *How to Get Started in Golf*.

Single Publisher

There are one or two specialist golf book publishers, and this category offers the collector a high standard of both new and reprinted books.

The Grant Books partnership of Bob and Shirley Grant was established in 1971. It built up a unique role in golf book sales, publishing and distribution. Their own publishing list is very specialized, with many fine books on the architectural side of golf, biographies and histories. All these books are published to the highest standards.

David Hamilton's Partick Press was established in 1984 to print new works on the history of golf by traditional methods. These limited editions are numbered and signed, and quarter leather binding editions were introduced from 1987 onwards. The following are Partick titles to collect:

- *Early Golf in Glasgow* (1985): An analysis of the neglected poem *Glotta* of 1721 describing golf on Glasgow Green. Student golf is involved, and it shows that early golf was not confined to Scotland's east coast. 250 copies, board covers, twenty-three pages, maps and facsimile.
- *Early Aberdeen Golf* (1986): Extracts and analyses the golfing material in Wedderburn's *Vocabula*, printed in Aberdeen in 1636. 350 copies, board covers, thirty-two pages.
- *Early Golf at St. Andrews* (1987): Uses the golfing content in Croft Dickinson's *Two Students at St. Andrews*, showing the prices, duration and variety of golf equipment available in the late 1600s. 350 copies, board covers, thirty-eight pages, facsimile.
- *Game at Goff* (1987): Reprints William Black's forgotten *The Glasgow* golfing poem of that name. Seventy copies only in a quarter leather edition, twenty-one pages. This is regarded as the rarest of the Partick Press books.
- *Early Golf at Edinburgh and Leith* (1988): Looks afresh at the *Account Book of Sir John Foulis of Ravelston* and the numerous golfing entries that give insight into play in the late 1600s before the foundation of the formal golf societies. Fifty copies in quarter leather, and 300 in the ordinary edition. Fifty-one pages, maps and illustrations.
- *The Sporting Padre* (1991): Describes the troubled life and downfall of the Rev. John Kerr, author of the classic historical works on Scottish golf and curling. Kerr's publication of his *Golf-Book of East Lothian* is examined from archival sources, and the provenance of many copies traced. Ninety copies in quarter leather, and 200 in the ordinary edition; forty-two pages, numerous illustrations, end-pocket with provenance list.
- *The South Sea Brithers* (1992): A light-hearted look at colonial golf at San Serriffe. The club song is perhaps by Edwin Morgan, and an end-pocket has dubious golfing ephemera from the early days of the island republic. 150 quarter leather copies, 150 ordinary binding; thirty-nine pages with wood engravings.

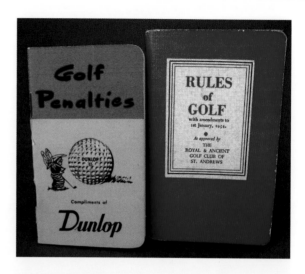

Such rules books are great value, and are not expensive at £10 each.

- *Golf – Scotland's Game* (1998): A full colour litho-printed publication for general sale. In addition, 350 copies were bound in quarter leather plus a slip case with an end-pocket containing a golfing map of Scotland and a bookmark stamped with Scottish club-maker's punches. 269 pages.
- *The Thorn Tree Clique* (2002): Contains the first line-by-line analysis of Mathison's Edinburgh poem *The Goff* of 1742, not only casting new light on the play, but revealing it as an Enlightenment parable. The four wood engravings are by Kathleen Lindsley, and an end-pocket has a facsimile of this rare and valuable poem. 280 copies were bound in quarter leather, plus slip case; in addition fifty deluxe copies were hand-tooled in leather, using a golfing motif.
- *Precious Gum*: The story of the gutta percha golf ball (2004). Seventy-nine pages, 450 copies presented in Solander case with quarter leather. Comes with gutta percha golf balls at three stages of production.

Charles Edmund Brock (1870–1938): *The Drive*, painted in 1894.

GOLF ART

Golf is not the force it once was in the art market. With troubles in the domestic economy of the golf-mad Japanese, and Valderrama now firmly established as a Ryder Cup venue, owners of 19th Century paintings no longer feel the same temptation to turn shepherds' crooks into mashie niblicks and place fluttering flagsticks among the dunes of anonymous coastal landscapes.

Antiques Trade Gazette, 31 January 2004

Golfing art comprises oil paintings, watercolours, drawings and prints. This sector of the market remains strong as long as it is an original, is well executed, is of a recognizable course or player, and is clearly signed. However, it is a fact that today's homes are smaller than in the past, many are flats and apartments, and we continue to downsize. Consequently, there is not so much wall-hanging space for our paintings and prints, and this social factor has affected the market.

Older Paintings and Their Prints

The vast majority of the classic paintings from the nineteenth century, featuring the very distinguished players and officials of the very earliest golfing societies and golf clubs, belong to those golf clubs today. A few are in the hands of private individuals, and they seldom come on

Charles Lees (1800–1880): *Summer Evening in Musselburgh Golf Links*.

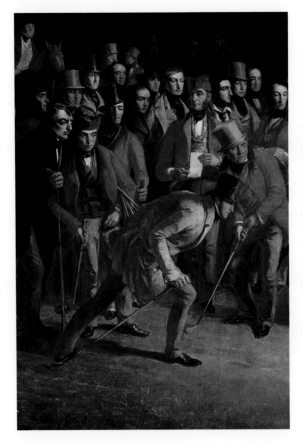

Charles Lees (1800–1880): The golfers in the left half of *The Golfers* painting, 1847.

The golfers in the right half of *The Golfers* painting, 1847.

to the market. For the golf historian, or even specialist golf collectors, these images afford a wonderful window through which to view the clubs and implements that were played with hundreds of years ago, the clothes and golfing attire that was either compulsory or fashionable to wear, the golf swing, the stance and the grip, the courses and how they have changed over time.

CHARLES LEES' *THE GOLFERS, A GRAND MATCH PLAYED ON ST ANDREWS LINKS*

Charles Lees R.S.A. painted his impressive piece *The Golfers, A Grand Match Played on St Andrews Links* in 1847. It was a game played by Sir David Baird and Sir Ralph Anstruther of Balcaskie on the one side, and Major Playfair of St Andrews and John Campbell of Glensaddell on the other. The painting was discussed in

Note the early iron club by Sir David Baird's heel at lower left.

Lemuel Francis Abbot (1760–1803): *The Blackheath Golfer*, the earliest known golf print featuring the uniformed William Innes, captain of the Blackheath Golf Club. First printed as a mezzotint engraving in 1790.

What every good caddie needs to keep his sanity: a bottle of the hard stuff!

Robert Browning's *History of Golf*, who observed that the painting dated from 'the golden age of foursome play (when) public interest was more excited over matches for high stakes between partnerships of well-known amateurs, than by contestants for silver Clubs or the stroke play competitions that succeeded them.'

Just look at the tension on the faces of the spectators in the gallery, many knowing that a small fortune would be made or lost if Major Playfair's feather ball dropped into the hole! There are at least two gentlemen in the gallery holding notebooks for bets, and in all likelihood they are refining the odds as the game progresses. The dress of the players and the gallery is just

as one would expect from the middle of the nineteenth century: top hats and jackets/coats, and the ladies in long dresses and bonnets. The caddies are holding large bunches of clubs, the majority of them being wooden long nose clubs. These are elegant and slim-necked because the feather ball was, of course, still in general use and the gutta-percha ball only just in circulation.

L.F. ABBOT'S PORTRAIT OF WILLIAM INNES

Another classic painting is Lemuel Francis Abbot's portrait of William Innes (1719–1795), a leading figure in the Blackheath 'Society of Goffers' that was a direct

David Allan (1744–1796):
William Inglis.

Look at the length of that club head!

forerunner of the Royal Blackheath Golf Club. Standing behind him is his caddie, dressed in the pensioner's uniform of the Greenwich Naval Hospital. Again, what a great opportunity to look at the wonderful golfing detail afforded us by Abbot. The subject of the portrait Innes carries a very large-headed long nose wood over his right shoulder, holding it on the slope as if it were a ceremonial sword. His 'uniform' comprises a red jacket with rather ostentatious golden shoulder epaulettes, very naval, and look at those glittering gold or gilt coat buttons, probably embossed with the Blackheath details.

His caddie carries a bundle of very early-looking woods and irons under his arm. Again, look at the size of the heads of the woods, and the two square toe

irons, which, if they were miraculously to materialize and go to auction today, would fetch at least £25,000 each! The caddie also has what is probably a large-sized feather golf ball partially hidden in his hand; the ball was to reduce its diameter over the next sixty years until it lost its place in the game.

PORTRAITS OF HENRY CALLANDER AND WILLIAM INGLIS

In 1812, Abbot painted another distinguished golfer, Henry Callander, who was the Blackheath Golfing Society captain in 1790, 1801 and 1807. What is noticeable is the length of the wooden club that he is holding. Also there are fashion points similar to those of

Sir George Chalmers' portrait of William St Clair of Roslin.

Who thinks that golf gloves are a modern invention?

the Innes painting. David Allan's painting of William Inglis in 1784 shows him holding a wooden club that comes up to his rib cage and its length is longer than his hand! In the background there is a uniformed official carrying aloft the Honourable Company of Edinburgh Golfers' Silver Club adorned with silver golf balls. Two drummers either side just add to the wonderful scenes indeed.

SIR GEORGE CHALMERS' PORTRAIT OF WILLIAM ST CLAIR OF ROSLIN

In 1771, Sir George Chalmers completed his portrait of William St Clair of Roslin. He was the four-time captain of The Honourable Company of Edinburgh Golfers and three times R & A captain. His jacket, compared to the one worn by William Innes, is more subdued. There are no epaulettes or chevrons on the sleeve and the jacket

LEFT: William Mosman (early to mid-seventeenth century) is best known for his Sir James and Sir Alexander MacDonald painting. The original hangs in the Scottish Portrait Gallery, Edinburgh.

Feather ball, red underlisting, and elegant club head – can't get much better!

buttons are covered in cloth. Who thought that the golf glove was a modern invention? Look at his right hand (not left) and there is a thin kid glove. In those days it was vogue to cut away the thumb and forefinger of the glove to afford better touch and feel!

THE RELEVANCE OF OLD GOLF ART

What else can the old golf masters show us today? Well, how about how the famous golf courses, such as St Andrews, have changed over the generations; or how the teeing areas have greatly improved; how the holing-out area became well cut putting greens; how famous landmarks, such as the red-brick university building suddenly appeared by the R & A clubhouse, or where the sheds were replaced on the Road Hole with

the building of thenew hotel. Another example is Lionel Percy Smythe's painting of Felixstowe Ferry Golf Course in 1904, which shows a part of the course that is no longer there due to soil erosion.

What, then, is the relevance today of old golf art? Probably today's average club golfer would have little or no interest in some of the classic pieces of art from the past, particularly as many of these famous paintings have been reproduced in print form throughout the centuries. And in all honesty, why would they want to hang a print of the 'Grand Match' or the 'Blackheath Golfers' in their home, especially as wall space is at a premium? Nevertheless, there is still a market for these prints, albeit much reduced when compared to years gone by.

Sir Francis Grant (1803–1878):
John Whyte-Melville.
The caddie carefully places
John Whyte-Melville's feather
ball on to a pile of sand, ready
for driving off.

The Next Generation of Golf Artists

There were many great paintings commissioned in the nineteenth and twentieth centuries; here are just three of them.

One of the great watercolour artists was John Smart RSA, born in Leith in 1838. His book/folio entitled *The Golfing Greens of Scotland*, in association with George Aikman ARSA, is superb and valuable (at auction it sells for between £8,000 and £12,000). Smart became an Associate of the Royal Scottish Academy in 1871. He died on 1 June 1899 in Edinburgh.

One of the greatest of all golf artists was Francis Powell Hopkins (Shortspoon was the 'brush name' of Major F. P. Hopkins); he was born in 1830 and died in 1913. He did work very successfully in oils, but preferred the freedom and spontaneity of watercolour, usually painting on blue paper.

Sir Francis Grant PRA, 1810–1878, is best known for his painting of John Whyte-Melville of Bannochy & Strathcainess, Captain of the R & A, in 1823. Historically, the Whyte-Melville painting may be one of the most important in the R & A's superb collection because of the artist and subject involved. It was painted in 1873. Whyte-Melville was one of the foremost members of the R & A throughout the nineteenth century, even to the extent that he was given the honour of laying the foundation stone for the clubhouse in 1853.

TERMS USED IN ART AND PRINTING

ART TERMS

Acrylic: Oil paint with the addition of a plastic resin. Much favoured by late twentieth-century and contemporary artists, as it dries much more quickly than traditional oils.

En grisaille: Literally means 'in grey' – presenting the image in a monochrome. Much used by Michael Brown in his famous group of artwork for the Life Association of Scotland Calendars (1892–1916).

Gouache: The use of opaque watercolour, adding a form of gum to the watercolour. This method is often used for commercial artwork, such as originals for posterwork.

Giclée: Pronounced 'ghee-clay' and means in French 'spray of ink'. It was originally developed as a method of proofing (checking for quality and accuracy). Images of an original work of art can be captured digitally by computer, and these can be so good that the copy can be virtually identical to the original! Hundreds of inkjets spray a million droplets of ink per second on to the canvas that is spun on a drum. Once completed, an image comprises almost twenty billion droplets of ink and is the closest duplication of an original artwork that is humanly, mechanically or technically possible.

Silk screen: Also known as serigraphy. Ink or paint is brushed through a fine fabric screen, portions of which have been masked for impermeability for each colour.

Offset lithography: A photographic printing technique that uses inks carried by rubber rollers (blankets) to transfer images from metal or plastic plates to paper. The continuous tones of a design are converted into small dots of different sizes by means of an optical method called 'screening'. Whereas a newspaper would have sixty-five lines per 1in, art prints have a finer screen of up to 200 lines per 1in. For colour work, the colours are separated into red, yellow, blue and black tones before six plates are prepared. These plates, which are prepared through various chemical processes, will print the tiny dots in a specific colour according to the separations.

PRINT TERMS

Artist's proof: Additional prints not included as part of the regular limited edition.

Acid free: A descriptive term for specially made materials, used either for a print or in the framing process, that are free of acids, because acids can cause discoloration and damage to the print.

Counter signature: On a limited edition, the signature of the artist and, for example, the golfer in the picture, often adds historical and monetary value to the print.

Limited edition: A fixed number of identical prints of a painting, signed by the artist, sequentially numbered and showing both the print's number and the total edition size.

Open edition: Identical prints that are signed by the artist and published in an unlimited number.

Remarque: Usually an original drawing made by the artist in the margin of a limited edition print. Can add substantially to the value of a limited edition print.

Textured canvas: An image is printed by offset lithography on to a thin piece of material, and this is heated and bonded to the canvas. It replicates the look of an original painting, including texture and the artist's brush strokes.

RIGHT: *Michael J. Brown: his painting for the 1899 Life Association of Scotland calendar features a match between F. G. Tait, Leslie Balfour Melville, Ben Sayer and W. Auchterlonie.*

This original Michael J. Brown painting sold at auction for over £20,000 in 2006.

ART TERMS AS USED BY AUCTION HOUSES AND GALLERIES

The following terms are commonly used by auction houses and galleries in relation to artists and their art.

Craig Campbell: In our qualified opinion a work by the artist.

Attributed to Craig Campbell: In our opinion a work of the period, which may in part or whole be by the artist's hand.

Style of Craig Campbell: In our opinion a work of the period and style of the artist, but not by the artist.

C. Campbell: In our opinion a work not of the period or by the artist.

After Craig Campbell: In our opinion a work that is a copy of a work by the artist.

Signed: In our opinion the work is signed by the artist.

Bears signature: In our opinion the works bears a signature that may be that of the artist.

Dated: The work is dated, and in our opinion was executed at or about this date.

OPPOSITE, RIGHT: *The value of this Michael J. Brown print is enhanced because it is still complete with its 1901 Life Association of Scotland calendar.*

Twentieth-Century Artists

ARTHUR WEAVER

Probably the best golf artist of the late twentieth century is Arthur Weaver. He was born on 24 February 1918 in London, and was educated at the Hornsey School of Art (1934–1938). Upon his release from National Service in 1947 he moved to Wales, and took up teaching art at Cardiff School of Art and in the Adult Educational Settlements in the South Wales valleys. Arthur Weaver's forte is landscape work, and his paintings have ranged from depictions of railways, oil wells, scenes in the cotton fields, cattle for American cattle breeders, and the world's finest golf courses. He works mainly in watercolour, presenting favourite holes on famous golf courses: the observer can picture himself playing on the course. Weaver reached his zenith in the late 1960s and early 1970s, and his originals are much prized items today.

LINDA HARTOUGH

One often asked question when it comes to golf art is, who will be the new Arthur Weaver? I don't have the definitive answer, but there has been, and still is, a select group of modern artists, one of whom may well be that person. A front runner must be the American artist Linda Hartough, whose pictures, with their clarity and realism, regularly win her great praise.

She is one of a handful of artists to be commissioned by the USGA and the R & A in the same year, to do the annual official paintings and prints for their Opens. Her golf-painting career began in 1984, when Augusta National commissioned her to paint one of its holes, and she has never looked back. Her approach is to spend a week at the course, taking photographs at different times of the day in order to capture all possible lights. She then works out what it is that makes the hole stand out, and ensures she includes that in the painting.

KENNETH REID

There are several British artists, too, who may soon assume the title of best modern-day golf artist. Englishman Kenneth Reid was born in 1941; in 1962 he was made a Fellow of the Royal Society of Arts.

J. Douglas (1858–1911): *North Berwick*. A watercolour featuring golfers playing the twelfth hole of the West Links in 1907.

OLDER PRINTING TECHNIQUES

Aquatint: A copper or zinc plate is covered with porous wax, which creates a grained or toned pattern on the plate. The design is put on in the form of an acid-resisting varnish, followed by immersion in an acid bath. The acid eats away the wax and creates areas to receive the ink.

Chromolithograph: A perfection of lithography whereby a range of colours is introduced. It is a forerunner of 'off-set' lithography. This form was much used in the early twentieth century, and good examples are the *Vanity Fair* colour prints, Charles Crombie's *Rules of Golf*, and the amusing prints of golfers drawn by noted artists such as Lionel Edwards, Louis Wain and Cecil Aldin.

Copperline: A sharp tool called a 'graver' or 'burin' is used to gouge a line in the copper plate. The varying depth of the line determines the width of the printed line. Under the glass the beginning and end of an engraved line are noticeably pointed.

Engraving: Made by coating a metal plate with a wax material known as 'ground'. The engraver draws the image in the wax and exposes parts of the plate. The plate is then dipped in acid that burns the lines in the plate. Ink is then applied to the plate; it is wiped off the surface laving only the ink in the acid-formed lines. If the plate is copper, because this is a very soft material, only 200 to 250 impressions could be reproduced and only the first fifty or so were perfect;

after that the image became progressively blurred. Look for the impressed mark, an indentation made in the paper during this procedure, which surrounds the image. On a copper engraving this mark is rarely more than 1/4in (6mm) from the image itself. In the case of steel engravings, the mark may be 1 to 1 1/2in (2.5 to 3.5cm) from the image. Steel was much cheaper, and hundreds, if not thousands of impressions could be made from a plate before the image began to blur.

Etching: The metal plate is covered with a thin layer of a material impervious to acid, usually wax, and the image is drawn into this 'ground' with a sharp instrument. The plate is then dipped into the acid, which is allowed to 'bite' into the lines and other marks until they are deep enough to hold the required amount of ink. Areas intended to be lighter in tone could then be masked off and the plate again dipped into the acid, this time deepening only those elements of the image that were to be darkened. This is one of the earliest forms of reproduction of an image. Golf collectors can seek etchings of Dutch 'Kolfers' by such famous artists as Rembrandt. Although the current prices of such prints are expensive, they are very good value when compared to modern works.

Intaglio: The artist carves out the area that is to be printed. Ink is spread over the surface, and the ink is

LEFT: Francis Powell Hopkins (1830–1913): This is one of his famous paintings at Pau Golf Club in France.

The Rules of Golf *illustrated prints and their folio can be both art and a book.*

wiped off the raised area. The paper is pressed onto the inked surface. Intricate lines give the feeling of depth and texture. Dry point is the same, except that the remnants within the lines are not wiped off, and this gives the effect of a less sharp effect to the lines; some describe it as soft.

Mezzotint: The surface of the plate is roughened to create raised areas, and is regarded as being the ultimate type of print. Most mezzotints with colour have been water coloured after being printed with black ink.

Photogravure: A photographic process that does away with the lithographic dots. The copper plate is covered with a resin followed by a light-sensitive emulsion. The plate is exposed to a photographic transparency that usually contains grey tones. Following acid baths, the plate is created and ready for hand printing. There is just a very fine grain effect. Also known as 'photolithograph'.

BELOW: John I. McClymont: *Old Tom Morris 1821–1908.*

ABOVE LEFT: J. Hassall (1868–1948) was a prolific illustrator for various mediums such as prints, ceramics and postcards.
ABOVE RIGHT: J. Hassall (1868–1948): *The Lie.*

COLLECTORS' HELPFUL HINTS

- Is the painting or print signed, dated and titled by the artist? If yes, then that is as good as it gets.
- Look at the back of the painting, or at the back or the frame for information on its past history – an auction label or the name and address of an art framer.
- Check the Art Price Index, easily available on the Internet for information on the artist, what originals or prints have been recorded, and what prices realized.

Originally he specialized in watercolours of British Isles courses, but he became noted at the Open at St Andrews in 1984. In 1996, Reid decided to devote all his energies to his golf art, and in the same year he was commissioned by the Championship Committee of the R & A and the USGA to create the official posters for their respective Open Championships.

GRAEME BAXTER AND CRAIG CAMPBELL

Then there are two Scotsmen, Graeme Baxter and Craig Campbell. Graeme Baxter is one of the world's most highly acclaimed artists of golfing landscapes. His work is admired and prized internationally for its superb quality, depth of feeling and knowledge of the subject.

One aspect that sets Craig Campbell apart from his contemporaries is his age (forty-five), and his skills as both a landscape and portrait artist. His strict mantra is that the eye is the key to a successful portrait. He was born in Prestwick, Scotland, in 1960 and studied graphic design at the Glasgow College of Art. Thought by many to be the outstanding British golf artist of his generation, his reputation as a leading sports artist was strengthened by a number of prestigious

TOP: Arthur Weaver (b.1918): *The 8th on the New Course, St Andrews*, painted in 1989.
BELOW: Two paintings by Craig Campbell: *above:* Tiger Woods on the last day of the 2005 Masters.
Right: Francis Ouimet on his way to winning the 1913 US Open.

A TRUE STORY

As reported in the *Antiques Trade Gazette*, 31 January 2004:

The work of the Scottish miniaturist... this 11½ x 9 inch watercolour showed the future Rear Admiral Robert Wauchope standing by an unmissable putt on an unidentified Scottish golf course [believed to be either Leith or Bruntisfield]. The painting was signed and dated 1803 or 1808, placing it in an extremely rare group of signed and dated depictions of golfers from the pre-Victorian era. ... Given that the course on which he was standing was unidentified and that prices for golfing pictures have cooled in recent years, a number of people regarded a pre-sale estimate of £5,000–£7,000 for what was, at the end of the day, a fairly small watercolour, as realistic enough...

The painting was sold for £56,000!

OPPOSITE TOP: Heath Robinson (1872–1944) is best known for his over-the-top conceptual inventions and contraptions.

ABOVE: Graeme Baxter: *Cruden Bay 1998* – the course looks mouth-wateringly inviting!

Graeme Baxter: *Turnberry 1996* – the landmark hotel overlooking the venue for the 2009 Open.

exhibitions, including a tour of the USA and a show at the 1994 Open Championship.

His attention to detail and mastery of colour has won him many admirers. Patrons of his work include HRH The Duke of Kent, Curtis Strange, Fred Couples, Sandy Lyle, Sam Torrance and Bernard Gallagher. Only time will tell, but certainly the images of golf as portrayed by these artists are safe in their hands!

Buying an Original Painting

When you buy an original painting, whether old or new, here are some considerations:

- Is the artist still alive? If he was a well liked artist then there is a good chance that his surviving works will appreciate.
- What of the artist's qualifications? Was he a member of such august societies as the Royal Academy (RA), RSW (Scottish Watercolours), RSA? Google is a good search engine to do some research on the artist or the subject matter.
- And, most importantly, do you like the subject matter?

Buying a Limited Edition Print

When you buy a limited edition print, here are some considerations:

- How many limited edition prints were produced?
- Do you know for certain that the plates have been destroyed to stop a printing in future years?
- Is the print numbered, and does it state how many were produced (e.g. 34/100)?
- Has the artist signed the print, or is it a facsimile?
- Has the artist added any attractive remarques to the border? Arthur Weaver was a keen advocate of this way of personalizing and, to a certain degree, making each print individual.
- Is the print mounted and/or framed, as these are extra costs?
- And, most importantly, do you like the subject matter?

To protect your investment use conservation glass that affords UVF protection and be careful not to have them subjected to direct light or fluorescent lights.

BUYER BEWARE

LOST BALL

✳ An eighteenth- or early nineteenth-century print should not be composed of dots.

✳ Some prints are dipped into strong tea or coffee to make them appear old and stained.

✳ Oil paintings and watercolours have their problems, too. New oil paintings can be made to look old, either by putting them into old frames, or by slightly distressing the canvas.

✳ Fakes made by the giclée process are causing havoc in the art world.

✳ In some instances a golfing theme may have been added to an old oil or watercolour to increase its appeal (hence the introductory quote from the *Antiques Trade Gazette*). The obvious ones are where a flag has been placed on a flat area within the landscape, and to the uninitiated eye just looks like a remote golf hole. Another con is to place a golf club into the hand of, say, a young lady. Check the symmetry of the painting, because the addition will often make the painting look unbalanced.

✳ When buying an old print, get it out of its frame. The seller may raise their eyebrows and wring their hands, but don't let that put you off. The back of the print, with its look and feel, should confirm almost immediately whether it is a fake or the real article. Look at the image under a glass: you don't want to be seeing dots; is it an early impression i.e. the image is clear and sharp, not blurred? Is the image black and white, or has it been hand coloured? And what of the backing? Does it retain its original frame, or maybe it was reframed a long time ago. And do you like the subject matter?

✳ Look out for 'mounted on backing paper' or lined, as this means that something amiss may have happened to the piece of artwork.

✳ With prints and engravings, check to see that the border has not been cropped or cut off.

✳ Often the border will have an impressed mark from the engraver or printer, and the loss of the border can devalue a print by some 70 per cent.

✳ Modern prints and pictures can be deliberately distressed to make them look old – which is one very good reason to buy from a reputable supplier such as a recognized art or antiques dealer, or an international auction house.

This large (36 x 24in / 90 x 60cm) advertising poster would be of interest to golf enthusiasts.

A hard-to-find Royal Crown Derby lady golfer, *circa* 1930.

GOLF'S OBJETS D'ART

Although golf clubs, balls and books dominate the hobby of golf memorabilia collecting, there has been always been a healthy level of interest in golfing ceramics and decorative golfing glassware. Ceramics and glassware came about as golfing trophies or as decorative arts complimenting the growth of the game, and were often awarded as alternatives to medals, spoons and silver trophies. Silver clubs belonging to the oldest golf societies were also played for: the winner would fix to the club a silver replica of the ball they had used.

A very early ceramic object d'art – even earlier than the Pitcairn Trophy – is a Chinese Export porcelain punch bowl dating to between 1745 and 1800. Chinese Export ware dominated the European market until the second half of the eighteenth century, when the expansion of porcelain manufacture in Europe replaced the expensive imported wares. Chinese Export porcelain was primarily decorated in hues of pink and is styled 'famille rose'.

Organizations and families of the landed gentry would order 'famille rose' porcelain through the British East India Company, giving the company a copy of their armorials or insignia, which would be sent to China to copy on to porcelain. This fine punch bowl is a superb example of this early ware, and surely can't be the sole survivor of a line of important wares! Keep a lookout.

There is a medallion painted on both sides of its exterior of a golfing figure with a golf club raised in full back swing. In the background there is an undulating golf course and a castle. This was taken from David Allan's drawing that formed part of the letterhead of the Honourable Company of Edinburgh Golfers. This bowl was part of a private collection of Chinese Export ceramics, and was sold at Sotheby's in

THE PITCAIRN TROPHY

In January 1994, Phillips auctioned an extremely rare early nineteenth-century Spode Imari-decorated punch bowl, its front inscribed in capitals: 'Bow of Fife Golfing Club Prize Medal for 1814 Won by John Pitcairn Esq of Kenneard.' It was conventionally decorated with peonies and leafage in underglazed blue and reds highlighted with gilt, a blue scroll and an insect-decorated border. The Bow of Fife is an area of land some five miles West of Cupar in Fife, and the Pitcairn family are still landowners in the area. The bowl measured 25in (63cm) long by 6in (15cm) high. The problem was that when Robert 'Bob' Gowland, the Phillips director in charge of golf, discovered it, it was in several pieces! Realizing just how important this piece of ceramic was, he had it professionally restored, and what a great job was done. Of course the catalogue noted that it had been repaired. This bowl is significant because it is the earliest recorded golfing non-medal prize. The bowl sold for £14,000.

This the earliest recorded golfing non-medal prize; it was sold at auction in 1994 for £14,000.

The ceramic figurine in the centre was a retail advertising item.

1988 for over £20,000; it is now part of the famed Valderrama Golfing Memorabilia collection.

Holland is often mooted as being the alternative country where the game of golf was developed. Certainly it spawned games played with clubs and leather balls, though more on ice than grass. During the sixteenth century, Holland became a centre of production for tin-glazed earthenware. While Harlem, The Hague and other cities had factories, it was at Delft that the leading potters produced the wares that bear the name of the city. During the seventeenth century, Delft was greatly influenced by the blue and white porcelain brought to Holland from the Far East by the Dutch East India Company.

The Delft factories produced blue and white tiles, some of which were themed with men playing a game called Het Kolven, or Colf. These are very popular with collectors today, and were usually framed for safekeeping and display. Unfortunately these are still being made, and can be found in their hundreds in souvenir shops in, for example, Amsterdam – and on occasions have been passed off as being a lot older

This Chinese Export porcelain bowl sold at auction in 1988 for over £20,000.

than they actually are! There are also larger blue and white tiles (6 x 8in/15 x 20cm), beautifully painted with detailed scenes of golf-type games being played on the ice.

Other rare early golfing items seen by the author include a ceramic church warden's pipe bowl that has been estimated to date to the 1700s. It was decorated in relief with crossed golf clubs, and measured 3in (7.6cm).

There was little activity by the ceramic makers until

Three mint Gerz golfing items still with their stoppers; they are hard to beat for condition.

the 1880s, when rather cynically they literally hopped on to the golfing bandwagon! They began decorating their basic ceramic pieces, such as tea services and other tableware, with hand-painted or applied transfers depicting Victorian or later Edwardian golfing scenes, male golfers typically dressed in red golfing jackets, plus fours, flat caps and tweeds, young caddies holding a bundle of wooden-shafted golf clubs under an arm, or beautiful young lady golfers.

Golf was a new and upwardly moving sport, and ceramic manufacturers saw a good opportunity to increase their sales, with little new investment. Some manufacturers would depict scenes of famous golf courses, while others would show famous golfers such as Old Tom Morris at the turn of the nineteenth century. Of course, today they are admired both for their attractiveness as well as in their role of being wonderful snapshots, letting us see what golfers were wearing, how they swung a club, and how the courses looked.

Golf-related ceramics is not just confined to tableware: look out for jardinières, baluster vases, classical two-handled vases, and even a Wedgwood plate that experts often erroneously claim to be depicting Neil Armstrong playing golf on the moon!

Since there is such a wide choice of design and manufacturers in these fields, it is a good idea to decide first of all what kind of china or glass you would like to col-

A fine Morrisan vase in reds, blacks and yellows.

lect. Is there a certain design, manufacturer or pattern that appeals to you? Some confine themselves to, for example, golfing teapots by just one, or by different makers; others may be drawn to a particular design, such as Doulton wares. Some collectors without the restrictions of a budget may want to collect only the very rarest pieces of ceramic or glass, with rarity based on colour variations, or just concentrate on rare Burslem blue and white ceramics.

ABOVE:
A wonderful
collection of
Schwartzburg
Rudolfstadt
ceramics.
RIGHT: Cheap
and cheerful
souvenir
mementos by
Arcadian,
Goss and
Grafton.

Some Popular Nineteenth- and Early Twentieth-Century Ceramic Manufacturers

GOSS

In 1887 W. H. Goss of Stoke-on-Trent introduced their new line of miniature souvenir ware to mark Queen Victoria's Jubilee on the throne. Adolphus Goss came up with the concept of reproducing miniature ceramics of famous antiquities that were found in local museums, and having these decorated and personalized with that town's coat of arms. The collecting of such souvenirs became a national craze in late Victorian and Edwardian times: they were everywhere, there were plenty of different shapes and themes to collect, and they were cheap. It was so popular that before 1914, some 90 per cent of British households contained some of this Goss-type crested china. The range was later extended to include ceramic salt- and peppershakers in the shape of bramble-patterned golf balls decorated with the coats of arms of various British towns and cities.

Similar to Goss was Grafton. The Grafton factory and their crested ware had a pleasing translucent appearance – in fact the experts rate Grafton as being the finest of all potteries to make crested ware. Grafton's rather pompous-looking golfing colonel with his rather disdainful expression may well have symbolized for non-golfers what a typical golfer looked like 100 years ago! A relatively inexpensive way of collecting would be to assemble the match-holders produced by Grafton, Arcadia and others.

LENOX

In 1889 Jonathan Caxon and Walter Scott Lenox founded Ceramic Art Co., in Lawrenceville, New Jersey. Caxon left in 1896, and in 1906 the company was renamed Lenox. The firm produced attractive golf items of various shapes and sizes between 1894 and 1906. The majority of items produced up to 1896 were of a male golfer in blue on a white background; post 1896, light and dark greens on a white background were introduced, and these proved to be very popular. Lenox also enhanced selected pieces with sterling silver rim bands.

Two views of a large Burslem vase, exquisitely hand painted.

Lenox pieces mostly carry the name or initials of the artist who produced the expert decoration found on its wares; a noted example was W. Clayton.

The following are some of the shapes and sizes to search for:

● a 14in (35cm) tall pitcher with and without gold wash trim on the rim;

A good Ceramic Art blue and white mug; steins have a lid.

Lenox continues to produce golfing items. One of their prize pieces would be the 1995 Masters limited edition plate decorated with gold edges and featuring the Augusta National Club House in its centre. These were only made for, and given to contestants, officials and long-standing members of the press.

SPODE

Josiah Spode founded the Spode factory in Stoke-on-Trent, Staffordshire in 1776. By the early 1800s it was producing top quality English bone china, and in 1813 Josiah's son went into partnership with W. T. Copeland. In more recent times the factory merged with the Worcester group. Copeland Spode mostly made blue or green stoneware containers such as jardinières and biscuit barrels with white relief. This type of ware with white relief is referred to as 'pate sur pate' – that is, with figures moulded in white clay and then fired to the body of the piece.

They also made teapots, jugs, mugs, creamers, pitchers, ornate decanters and three-handled steins such as the ones pictured. A very collectable Copeland Spode piece is its three-handled loving cup or tyg that measures just over 5in (12.7cm) high and 5in in diameter. Its colours are greys and cobalt blues, and there is gold trim applied to the outer surfaces of the three handles and the mug's rim. The golfing figures are depicted in white relief. There are three separate golfing scenes on the sides of the mug; one depicts a golfer approaching the green where a young caddie is in attendance.

- a miniature 3¹/₂in (9cm) tall oil lamp with handle and silver trim;
- a whisky jug 7in (18cm) high with a finger-hole handle and silver stopper with chain;
- mugs and steins (with lids) measuring 5¹/₂in (14cm), 5³/₄in (14.6cm) or 5⁷/₈in 15cm);
- three-handled toasting mugs, some with plain beaded and some with fancy rosette sterling silver trim, measuring in size from 3¹/₄in (8.2cm) – only one is known to exist – to 3⁷/₈in (9.8cm), 4in (10cm), 5¹/₄in (13.3cm), 5¹/₂in (14cm) and 6¹/₂in (16.4cm) – again, only two are known to exist. It has been estimated that Lenox produced fewer than 100 three-handled mugs. Look for the CAC mark on Lenox pieces.

Left to right: A Copeland late Spode biscuit jar with lid; a Kingsware mug; and a Copeland late Spode teapot.

Copeland Spode called this blue colour 'cobalt blue'.

ROOKWOOD

The Rookwood Pottery Co., of Cincinnati, Ohio, produced very few items with golf motifs; however, one extremely rare piece was their four-handled loving cup trophy, decorated with a border of matchstick-looking golfers. It was produced at the end of the nineteenth century, measured 7½in (19cm) high, and was finished in yellows, greens and browns. Not so rare are their art deco golfing pieces produced in the 1920s and 1930s. One item that has been found in reasonable numbers is a clever pop-up cigarette holder kept in a ceramic base. Sports figures in relief are presented on the outer surface, including a male golfer. These were executed in pastel blue, green and pink.

ROYAL DOULTON

Royal Doulton (the royal charter was granted in 1902) have always been prolific makers of golfing ceramics, with their ranges sporting – amongst others – golfers dressed as seventeenth-century Civil War opponents, either puritan Roundheads or royalist Cavaliers. This is strange, really, although at least James I and his son Charles I did play the game; it certainly would have been deemed too frivolous by Oliver Cromwell.

Their Bunnykins series featured charming graphics of golfing bunny rabbits taken from watercolours by Barbara Vernon. This range was aimed at mothers and their children in the 1930s; thus the majority of plates, bowls, jugs and cups were used extensively on the table, and sharp forks, knives and spoons scraped away

A wonderful Copeland Spode green stoneware container.

at the food, and so the transfer decoration on the chinaware was damaged.

Doulton's Burslem porcelain from the 1890s and early 1900s is immediately recognizable by its hand-painted blue-and-white colour schemes. Also, most of the Doulton Burslem pieces were signed or marked by the individual artist. Burslem remains one of the most expensive golfing ceramics sections to get into – although they are not expensive when considered together with other nineteenth-century ceramics.

Kingsware remains a very collectable range – strange to see Crombie's puritan figures playing such a frivolous game!

Doulton's Bradley Picturesque series comprised plates decorated with a golfing Cavalier figure with highly decorated borders in greens and yellows. Marked D1398, the range was launched in 1903.

Doulton Kingsware featured Crombie-type figures in relief on mainly jugs, pitchers and mugs, but also 'nineteenth hole' plates and dishes. The soft colour effect of dark browns and tan browns was achieved by the manufacturing technique of applying the decorative colours to the inside of the mould. When the terra cotta coloured slip was poured into the mould and fired, the colours were fused to the body of the object. Consequently the colour of the interior is the same colour as the background on the outside. Another decorative variation of Kingsware is known as 'Airbrush Brown' (D5716) – its more vibrant colours, such as reds and greens, were created when the items were decorated after the firing and before the glazing.

Doulton Queensware was produced for only a short time, and all golfing items are valuable.

Doulton Lambeth, made by Royal Doulton in the early 1900s, featured mugs, jugs, beakers and even a tobacco jar that were all decorated with golfers in white relief on a tan-coloured background, and decorative leafy borders usually in blues or browns. There were three Lambeth golfing scenes: *Lost Ball*, *Putting* and *Driving*. Also look out for a rare pair of Doulton Lambeth stoneware bookends modelled as caddies, one entitled *Fed Up* and the other *Foozled*.

Royal Doulton made their beautiful Morrisian ware (named after William Morris) at their Burslem factory, in the period 1900 to the 1920s. Golfing figures were dressed as bewigged and moustached Cavaliers (in strong contrast to the Puritan-style golfers in the Series Ware). Morrisian ware shapes included large vases, fern stands and jardinières, and its colour schemes were mainly reds, yellows and black. Occasionally Morrisian ware was made in blues and blacks, but these are very rare.

Doulton's most prolific range was Series ware: it comprised the basic cream-coloured stock that was then decorated with transfers and hand-tinted in various and many themes, one of which was golf. There were six Series ware ranges featuring golf:

1. Firstly the *Charles Crombie style golfers* from the Perrier *Rules of Golf* – the golfers are often described as Roundheads from the seventeenth-century English Civil War, or Quakers or New World pilgrims. They are

LEFT: It is rather incongruous to see 'Puritan' fellows playing such a frivolous game as golf on these Doulton Series ware ceramics.

ABOVE: A large 11in (28cm) two-handled Royal Doulton vase, and a Series ware quart jug with stopper.
RIGHT: This piece is one of the rarest Series ware, decorated with Crombie golfers.

always to be found in humorous and or unlikely golfing situations. Produced between 1911 and 1932, the most prolific pattern number was D3395. Shapes include bowls, serving dishes, platters, jugs, large two-handled vases, punch bowls, toothpick holders, sugar shakers, candlesticks and ashtrays. Each piece also featured a proverb in 'ye olde style' English:

- All fools are not knaves, but all knaves are fools.
- Every dog has his day, and every man his hour.
- Give losers leave to speak and winners to laugh.
- He hath good judgement who relieth not wholly on his own.
- He that always complains is never pitied.
- Promise little and do much.

Lambeth ceramics seldom come to auction these days – they are not easy to find.

Other pattern numbers were D2296, D3394 and D5960.

2. The second range was Royal Doulton's Series ware 'proverb' plates (D3391 and D3481), measuring up to 10in (25cm) in diameter; these were in production between 1911 and 1928. Each side plate or dinner plate featured a fancy-looking Cavalier playing golf, an ornate border, and a pair of proverbs, each different to the ones featured in the 'Crombie' Series ware:

- An oak is not felled by one blow. Take the will for the deed.
- Fine feathers make fine birds. Handsome is that handsome does.
- Fine feathers make fine birds. Old saws speak the truth.
- Hope springs eternal in the human breast. Hope

TERMS USED

Back stamp (known in America as a 'back mark'): Similar to the silver smith's hallmark or a firm's trademark. It identifies the series or range, and the company that produced the piece.

Bone china: Originally soft paste porcelain with the addition of calcined bones to form a hard, impervious body.

Ceramics: From the Greek 'Keramic', a generic term for all forms of pottery and porcelain.

Earthenware: Made from clay, quartz and feldspar. A porous pottery that requires glazing to make it waterproof.

Hard-paste: Hard-paste porcelain is fired at a higher temperature than soft paste.

Porcelain: A mixture of china clay and china stone that becomes hard, translucent and white when fired.

Tin glaze: An opaque tin oxide glaze used on earthenware, mainly Delftware.

Transfers: Redecorating, a method of printing ceramics that involves transferring a design from an inked engraving.

Seconds: Items that have been misfired in the kiln, or with other manufacturing defects as detected by the manufacturer's quality assurance department.

Sgraffito: The outlines were scratched on to the soft clay before the firing, and afterwards the earth-coloured background was sprayed on to the whole surface and the scratched shapes were then filled in with solid colours.

Soft-paste: Soft-paste porcelain is made from kaolin, powdered glass, soapstone and clay.

Stoneware: A heavier type of pottery fired at a high temperature used for domestic wares and commercial pottery. An example would be the stoneware tee jars *circa* 1900 for holding the sand on the teeing-up area. These are probably the only ceramic item directly linked to playing golf, as opposed to decorative or prize pieces.

The standing Doulton 'Proverb' plate was only made between 1911 and 1928.

deferred maketh the heart sink.
- If at first you don't succeed try again. A miss is as good as a mile.
- Nothing venture nothing have. A bird in the hand is worth two in the bush.
- Nothing venture nothing win. Count not your chickens before they are hatched.

3. The third range was Royal Doulton's 'Gibson' ware (patterns E2766 and E2727), introduced in 1904; it did not appear after World War I. Charles Dana Gibson is best known for his painting of a very attractive young lady golfer, known as 'The Gibson Girl'. Each Gibson piece, such as cups, saucers and small vases, featured one of eight quotations:

- Don't watch the player, keep your eye on the ball.
- From 10am to 6.45pm this dog has been kept out. Where is the SPCA?
- Fore.
- Golf – a good game for two.
- Is a caddie always necessary?
- One difficulty of the game – keeping your eye on the ball.
- The last day of summer.
- Who cares?

4. Royal Doulton's 'Bateman' range (D5813) comprised three typical Bateman humorous cartoons: 'An Irate Golfer', The Laughing Caddies' and 'The Smug Golfer'. Various steins, cigarette boxes and a very collectable octagonal-shaped dish were used. The Bateman line was in production sporadically between 1930 and 1950.

5. Uncle Toby 'Golf' was one of fifteen sports games played by Uncle Toby, and was featured on jugs and cabinet or display plates (known in America as 'rack'). Produced between 1909 and 1930, pattern numbers for these wares include D3111, D3121 and D3197.

6. The final Royal Doulton golfing series was 'The Nineteenth Hole' featuring two golfers having a drink after a game of golf. Produced between 1914 and 1930. Pattern numbers were D3755 and D3770.

In 1971 Royal Doulton released a highly glazed 'Toby' jug called 'Golfer'; its Doulton number was D6623. David Briggs, one of Doulton's top designers, created this character beer jug and based the character on W. J. Carey who in 1970 was the CEO of Doulton in the USA. It was such a good seller (and hence not valuable today) that it stayed in the range until 1995. In 1987 Doulton had three 'Golfer' jugs in their range: D6784 (limited edition of 1,000) was basically the same as D6623 but in a new painted guise; D6756 measured 4$\frac{1}{8}$in (10.3cm), and H1970 was 2$\frac{7}{8}$in (7.2cm).

RIGHT: A fine Simon Peter Gerz stoneware salt-glazed jug in cobalt blue.
FAR RIGHT: A Weller Dickens ware pottery vase.

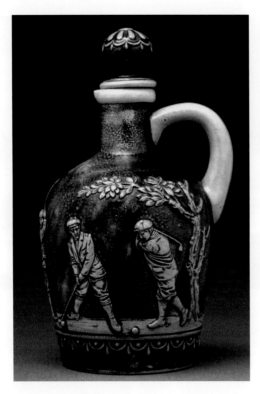

During the late 1980s and early 1990s Royal Doulton issued three new golfing figures. HN2992 was called 'Golfer' and was part of the 'Reflections' series, modelled as a 9¼in (23.4cm) high male golfer in a blue sweater; HN3276 was 'Teeing Off', a 9in (22.8cm) high male golfer; and in 1990 they released an 8in (20.3cm) high lady golfer putting. It was not marked on its base. There were other occasional pieces made at this time: for example, in 1984 DB32 Bogey Bunnykins, and in 1996 Paddington Bear Golfer (PB7).

In 2001, Royal Doulton in conjunction with Millennium Collectables made a Dunlop Caddie and Penfold Man, obviously based on the point of sale advertising figures made by Dunlop and Golf Ball Developments in the 1940s. Each limited edition figurine is hand-made, hand-painted and individually numbered (1 to 2,000) on its base. Possibly a great collectable for the future!

WELLER

One of the few, and probably the best known, American producers of golfing ceramics was the Weller Pottery, in Zanesville, Ohio. Its famous Dickens ware (named after Charles Dickens) stoneware series was produced at the turn of the nineteenth century. Their vases and jugs with golfing figures and scenes are relatively common but remain expensive to buy; their beer mugs are very rare. Dickens ware is almost always executed with a matt finish; ones with a high glaze finish are very rare. The decoration was applied by the sgraffito method. Lady golfing figures are harder to find than male figures; of the female golfers, some have a flying cape. Figures with white faces, as opposed to flesh tone, are rare and highly prized by Weller collectors.

OTHER CERAMIC MANUFACTURERS AND DESIGNERS

Amphora: Turn-Teplitz, Bohemia. An Austrian manufacturer of golfers and caddies often sporting inane grins and wearing rather inappropriate rain- or trenchcoats and outsized boots. Sometimes found without clubs in the bag and with variations in the decoration of the caddy's coat.

Arcadian Works: Stoke-on-Trent (originally Arkinstall & Sons). Made a vast selection of cheap golfing souvenir mementos in the shapes of golf balls, clubs

Left: A decorative Adagio china urn, hand painted by Malcolm Harnett in the 1990s.
Right: The ever-popular Burleigh ware 'Golfer' jug of tapering shape, circa 1930s.

Four attractive Crown Ducal pieces – note their strong bright colours.

and golf bags, decorated with transfers reflecting, for example, the name of the sea-side resort. Similar to the pieces made by Goss.

Atholware: Made a brown pottery jug with a silver lustre rim in the 1920s.

Belleek Pottery: Fermanagh, Northern Ireland. Founded in 1863 and has produced occasional golfing pieces.

Bing & Grondahl: Copenhagen, Denmark. This fact-ory is noted for its twentieth-century figures decorated in hues of blues and greys, and fired with a high gloss glaze. Made a collectable series of porcelain plates for the Memorial Tournament in the 1970s and 1980s.

Brain, E., & Co.: Fenton, Staffordshire. Produced Foley golfing plates, cups, saucers and beakers during the late nineteenth century.

Brannam, C. H.: Barnstaple, Devon. Made blue pottery jugs with golfing mottos.

Bridgwood: Staffordshire. Known for their golfing plates 'Golf Language', 'Them's Mushrooms' and 'The Indispensable Caddy'.

Burgess & Leigh: Burslem, Staffordshire. The Burleigh Golfer jug *circa* 1930s with its tapered golf handle, as a golfer is very popular with Art Deco collectors. The golf collectors often spurn the piece because of its garish colours, and tend to 'undervalue' it.

Carlton ware: *See* Wiltshaw & Robinson.

Chikaramachi: Japan. Made a limited number of golf items in the 1930s.

Coalport Porcelain Works: Coalport, Shropshire. Established 1750. Stoke-on-Trent from 1926. Made a pair of golfing figurines, 'First Tee' and 'Ladies Day'. In 1991 Coalport produced golfing plates known as 'Golfing Classics' featuring famous courses; each was a 10,000 limited edition.

Crown Ducal: *See* A. G. Richardson & Co.

Crown Staffordshire porcelain: Fenton, Staffordshire: this company made a selection of bone china golfing items during the 1930s. Another popular piece is of Young Tom Morris standing by a tree holding a golf club. Its Queensbury breakfast set was decorated with Bateman-type cartoon golfers. The firm was restyled Crown Staffordshire China Co. in 1948.

Dartmouth Pottery: Dartmouth, Devon. From 1947 made a mug decorated with a golfer in relief and a handle partially shaped as a golf bag, in colours to include browns and creams and yellows and cream. Watch out for reproductions, which will lack the Dartmouth stamp.

Derby Crown Porcelain (Royal Crown Derby): Produced a charming lady golfer in the late 1920s and early 1930s.

Fielding & Co.: Originally established in Devon, but from 1911 based in Stoke-on-Trent. Their Crown Devon series there was a golf ball salt and pepper set, marked 'Fore'. There is doubt that this factory produced the soft paste version of the Blackheath Golfers. Certainly it is 'Staffordshire' in the generic term. This model was produced in the latter half of the twentieth century and should never be accepted or passed off as earlier, in the manner that some modern Staffordshire has

been presented by unscrupulous dealers or on some on-line auction sites.

Foley: *See* E. Brain.

Gerz, Simon Peter: Hohr-Grenzhausen, Germany. The Gerz line was of blue and grey stoneware with applied figures that were salt-glazed and fired. Pieces included mugs, pitchers and jugs in a variety of shapes and sizes. Mugs and pitchers were usually produced with pewter lids attached to the upper part of the handle. Jugs typically had matching-colour stoneware stoppers with corks. One of their rarer pieces was a somewhat squat humidor.

Ginori, Richard: Italy, *circa* 1930s.

Goebell: Austria. Still trading. Their popular cruet set comprises a salt and pepper in the shape of golf balls.

Gorringes: Made golf-decorated breakfast cups and saucers.

Grimwades: Stoke-on-Trent. The Grimwades' Winton Ware comprised a set of six differently decorated dinner plates, and are fine examples of the colour-printing process on porcelain. 'The Golf Critics' series, with their pretty decorated borders, are particularly collectable today, and some of the humorous titles include 'A Full Swing' and 'The Indispensable Caddy'. Identical plates with the same border patterns have been noted with the Bridgwood factory mark to the base. Sporting Brownies is another popular collectable…but as someone once wrote, 'I never met one as a boy scout!'

Hauber & Reuther: Freising, near Munich, Bavaria, Germany. The HR factory produced steins in an amazing variety of shapes, sizes and colours. All were designed to be fitted with pewter lids, again attached to the upper handle. The scenes were etched and were typically of a single male golfer. Backgrounds were of varying scenes and colours.

Hummel: Germany. A popular item is the trinket dish with two rather chubby golfing children. Trade mark is a bee.

Jonroth Studios: Germany. Hand-painted ceramic golf plates.

Keele Street Pottery: Tunstall, Staffordshire. Made a range of golf mugs.

Limoges: Paris, France. Their golfing mugs were decorated with Edwardian-style men and women golfers.

ABOVE: Schwarzburg remains one of the most desirable ranges to collect.
RIGHT: A Schwartzburg Rudolfstadt porcelain golfing vase.

Lladro: Valencia, Spain. Pale blues and whites are popular in their ceramics that have from time to time featured a male and a lady golfer in their ranges.

Mason: Fenton, Staffordshire. Made plates in the late nineteenth century with a golfer on what looks like a tapestry or embroidery background; these are known as 'sampler' plates. Very collectable.

McIntyre: Began in Burslem, Staffordshire in 1860. Taken over by Moorcroft in the early 1900s. Continued to produce golfing tableware until the late 1920s. Between the 1890s and early part of the twentieth century, McIntyre made a teapot decorated with a male golfer dressed in red jacket and plus fours.

Minton: Stoke-on-Trent, Staffordshire. Makers of quality golfing plates and pitchers.

New York & Rudolstadt Pottery Co.: Rudolstadt, Germany. Another prolific producer of golfing ceramics was Schwarzburg, the trade name for New York & Rudolstadt Pottery. Produced from 1882 to 1932 in Rudolstadt, Germany, the Schwarzburg line includes a

wide variety of colourful pieces, primarily plates, vases and cups in many different sizes and shapes. The best known of the line show the infamous 'Christie Girl' in the centre, with other figures behind her. Numerous other cups and plates, 'signed' by 'Brown', show a variety of golfing figures on the golf course. Another famous artist was Harrison Fisher.

Noritake: Nagoya, Japan. Produced items mainly for the American market in the early to mid-1920s. Usually marked with a stylized insect in a circle with or without 'Noritake'. Still producing.

O'Hara Dial Co.: Waltham, MA, USA. They bought steins with plain pewter lids from Lenox, and then used their watch-making skills to decorate and enhance the lid tops with engravings. Obviously as they are basically Lenox pieces, they are in green on white backgrounds; however, a few rare pieces were decorated in an orange/brown colour scheme.

Owens, J. P., Pottery Co.: Zanesville, Ohio. Founded in 1885, and although well known for their art ware, there was a well heeled Edwardian male golfer, complete with handlebar moustache, in their range at the end of the century.

Pearce, A. B., & Co.: Ludgate Hill, London. In the

Susie Cooper pieces have been faked recently, so 'buyer beware' and be knowledgeable!

1910s, made china cups and saucers depicting golfers and caddies.

Richardson, A. G., & Co.: Gorden Pottery, Stoke-on-Trent. Established in 1915. Produced the Crown Ducal line of ceramics, beginning in 1915. The golfing line included a wide variety of colourful and humorous pieces including plates, bowls, mugs, vases, humidors. The scenes are typically of a struggling golfer with a caddie snickering in the background, and are comprised of hand-painted transfers and backgrounds. Their bright colours help these pieces display well.

Royal Bonn: Bonn, Germany. Founded by Franz Anton Mehlem in 1836. Producers of hand-painted porcelain or earthenware beer mugs and steins in the late nineteenth century.

Royal Worcester: Originally the Worcester Royal Porcelain Co. In recent times they have produced a 'Golfing Collection' of wall plates signed by Melvyn Buckley.

Sèvres: France. Producers of hand-painted porcelain

ABOVE: Three pieces from the Taylor Tunnicliffe factory.
RIGHT: A rare and valuable Arthur Wood biscuit jar
with rope-twist gilt metal handle and silver lid in
pristine condition.

circa late 1930s. Its golfing items seldom come to the market.

Shelley Potteries: Longton, Staffordshire. Originally the name 'Shelley' was used by Wileman & Co. Founded in 1925. Known for its golfing child signed and titled by Mabel Lucie Attwell.

Sleepy Eye: Winconsin, USA. A stoneware group of tablewares, rather crudely decorated in blues and produced during the Depression era to merchandise baking or cooking flour.

Susie Cooper China Ltd: Burslem, Staffordshire. Miss Cooper (Mrs C. F. Barker), like Clarice Cliff, is regarded as one of the twentieth-century great lady Art Deco ceramic designers. She is famous for two golfing scenes, one looking down the fairway and the other on the tee. Both are much sought after and therefore expensive. Renamed 'Susie Cooper Ltd' *circa* 1961.

Taylor, Tunnicliffe & Co: Founded in 1868 by Thomas Taylor and William Tunnicliffe for the purpose of making specialized pottery articles. Look out for tobacco jars and such items as a salad bowl with matching servers, their handles very finely painted with scenes reminiscent of Old Tom about to play a shot.

Warwick Wheeling: Virginia, USA, *circa* 1920s.

Wedgwood, Josiah: Stoke-on-Trent. Wedgwood made a product called 'Kenlock Ware' *circa* 1900. It was a red- or black-bodied stoneware, usually in the form of a small vase, painted with a figure of a lady golfer. Also 'Jasperware', a form of pottery with a coloured body, normally blue or black, occasionally green or purple, having applied decoration in white relief. Often on

Royal Doulton's Dunlop Man is a likely golf antique of the future.

ABOVE: Morrisian ware: it is a little strange that the lady's fashion is nineteenth century and the men's is seventeenth century!

LEFT: Morrisian ware is scarce, but the piece in blue is rare.

The evolution of the golf swing, as portrayed on golfing ceramics.

This Doulton Lambeth pitcher was made in 1900, and features three different turn-of-the-century golfing scenes.

This Royal Doulton Kingsware earthenware pitcher measures just over 9in (23cm).

tablewares and special pieces such as commemorative and souvenir products, or special commissions for the Ryder Cup. The Sports Series plates *circa* 1930s are very rare as only a few (less than twenty-five) were made before the series was cancelled. Its Etruria series of plates were also made at the same time.

Willerdy and Boch: Dresden. Made hand-painted plates in the early 1900s.

Williamson, H. M. & Sons: Longton, Staffordshire. Founded in 1879. In the early 1900s they made several golf pieces to include a sandwich plate, sugar bowl and milk jug. The former was decorated with an image of The Triumvirate in 1912.

Willow Art China: Longton, Staffordshire. Famous for its bust of Old Tom Morris decorated with a transfer usually of St Andrews, and aimed at the ever-expanding tourist industry at the turn of the nineteenth century. Also made cups, plates and saucers during the 1920s.

Wiltshaw and Robinson: Stoke-on-Trent: Their

Carlton Ware golf range depicted three figures – a golfer in red jacket, tweed cap and plus fours, another golfer dressed in brown, and a boy caddie standing between them – and the emblem 'Far & Sure'. The most common pieces of Carlton ware are the round match-stick holder and the tobacco jar or biscuit jar with a sil-ver-plated lid or cover. During the 1990s, fakes appeared of their four differently coloured golfing fig-ures that resembled the Dunlop Caddie.

Wood, Arthur: Longport, Staffordshire. Formerly Capper & Wood. Between 1904 and 1928 produced various earthenwares decorated with golfers, including a mug featuring a caddie in the 1930s and a bunny golfer cruet set.

Wood & Wood: The various Wood factories include Wood & Wood, and Wood & Son. Used stencil and hand-painted decorations to the figures of a male and lady golfer. An example is their biscuit barrel with lid.

GLASS TERMS

Etching: The glass is coated with a wax, and the decorative pattern is then drawn into the wax. Acid is applied, and the wax prevents it from affecting any unintended areas.

Engraving: A sharp instrument removes pieces of glass to form the design.

Cut glass: Created by initially cutting into the blank; this is followed by smoothing techniques, and finally polishing.

Intaglio: Cut or engraved decoration on glass.

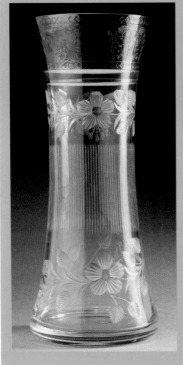

A large De Passe cut and acid-etched vase with silver overlay golfing scene in relief.

A pair of Bohemian glass golfing vases – the ultimate in decorative glassware.

Glassware

Golfing glass items are relatively affordable and fun to acquire as the focus of a collection or part of a broader collection. The majority of collectable golf glass was produced between 1890 and 1940 in England or the United States, and many of the items served a purpose such as drinking or smoking. As with their ceramic counterparts, some glass pieces were commissioned as competition prizes, or made exclusively for wealthy clients of glass companies. Collecting glassware is not so clear-cut (please excuse the pun) compared to collecting ceramics, because in the main they are not marked with the manufacturer's name. Collectors tend to concentrate their efforts on buying favourite shapes or pieces, rather than glass made by, for example, Hawkes. Dating can be helped when the piece has been decorated with a Sterling silver hall-marked accessory such as a rim to a glass decanter.

Glassware is decorated by etching, engraving or cutting. Cut-glass items were also available, with a second colour added by overlay, flashing or staining. In addition, enamelling was used to create multi-coloured designs on the surface of the glass, and these all added to the attractiveness and collectability of the item.

Look out for all sorts of glass, from clear to coloured to frosted. Decorations vary from hand-painted golfing scenes and golfers, to ones created by transfers (called 'decals' in America). Glass was also frequently decorated with silver overlays, some with silver rims and other edging, while others were partially or entirely overlays with silver. These should always be hall marked, or should at least state that it is Sterling silver.

Glassware items range from decanters, wine glasses, wine jugs, pitchers, ice buckets, cocktail shakers, silver

and glass combinations such as cruet sets with glass-cut mesh guttie salts and peppers, ladles, and so on.

Most companies producing glassware with a golf motif were American, while perhaps the rarest is the Austrian company Loetz.

AMERICAN COMPANIES PRODUCING GOLFING GLASSWARE

T. G. Hawkes & Co.: T. G. Hawkes & Co. was founded in 1880 in Corning, New York, and was perhaps the most prolific producer of golfing glassware in the early 1900s. Their pieces were primarily a line of barware including wine bottles, ice buckets, cocktail shakers and Martini pitchers in various sizes. Rims, lids and handles were offered in sterling and silver plate at different

A stunning collection of Hawkes golfing glassware: see you at the 19th hole!

costs. The pieces were typically intricately engraved with a golfing scene, wrapped around the body, showing grass, trees, birds, greens and a clubhouse. Most of the larger pieces have '19th Hole' engraved at the top. Other, rarer pieces include lidded cookie jars and boxes, and a round water jug with handle and spout.

Pieces are typically marked 'HAWKES', usually on the base and on the silver accents, and with the Hawkes' 'trefoil' (like a three-leaf clover with 'Hawkes' inside), usually, but not always, on the base. Markings are often missing due to age rubbing, but the scenes and craftsmanship are unmistakable. Other Hawkes pieces are

LEFT: A matching pair of Handel 'tobacco' and 'cigars' jars. BELOW: An uncommon Cambridge Glass Company amber-coloured glass jug with an acid-etched golfing scene, *circa* 1920s.

more simply designed – with the '19th Hole' engraving, but without the golf course scene. A very few pieces are found with coloured glass. Production declined after the war, and Hawkes went out of business in the 1960s.

Handel: The Handel Company operated out of Meriden, Connecticut. Founded in 1885, it continued operating until 1936. Their pieces were typically made of milk glass – an opaque white glass – with hand-painted transfer decorations and scenes. Their more colourful pieces were vases, typically with red/orange overtones and with ornate metal handles and bases, and humidors, with metal banding and hinges. These were usually decorated with a lady golfer in a red top and flowing white skirt. Most pieces are marked in capitals with 'Handel' on the bottom, are subject to wear, and are sometimes signed by the artist. Exceptionally rare pieces are signed 'P. J. Handel', one of the founders of the company, in what appears to be gold ink.

Other Producers: Other well known American companies producing golfing glassware in the early 1900s include the Cambridge Glass Company, Heisey, and the C. F. Monroe Company, best known for its Wavecrest line. Perhaps more commonly seen, however, is an amazing variety of unmarked clear and coloured glassware, usually barware – pitchers, decanters, bottles and even flasks – with sterling overlay golfing scenes. Glass

colours include blue, green and red, and the sterling overlay scenes range from simple to incredibly ornate.

SOME GLASS MAKERS THAT HAVE MADE GOLFING PIECES

Art Deco Co.: USA *circa* 1920s.

Black, Starr & Frost: New York. An important retailer like Tiffany, established in 1875.

COLLECTORS' HELPFUL HINTS

GLASS

- As with all areas of glass collecting, clear glass is more easily found. Coloured pieces are usually harder to find and as a result command higher prices.

- Unlike ceramics, broken glass is difficult to repair invisibly and thus is often discarded. Look out for damaged glass that has been hidden or disguised behind a frame or mount. You can not fix damage to glass; glue always looks unsightly. Sometimes it may be possible to smooth out a ragged edge by careful grinding; however, it should only be done by a professional as the glass object will easily disintegrate.

- Glass in the shape of a golfer is better than a piece of ordinary glass.

- If the piece looks as if it should have had a lid, stopper or top, ask where it is. If it is missing, this will adversely affect the value.

CERAMICS

- Once the collector recognizes and understands the manufacturer's marks on the base, check they are not 'seconds' marks, possibly indicating an inferior product.

- A popular theme for ceramic collectors has always been the collecting of teapots and plates, so the golf enthusiast will face stiff opposition in those fields.

- Cracks can be detected by black light – a light bulb held near to the area suspected of being damaged or repaired; the glazed area cannot be replicated.

- Colouring and glazing in reproductions or fakes are often different.

- To save on cost, fakes often lack the weight or gravitas of the real thing.

- Ceramics can be repaired and restored, but it is relatively expensive.

- Ceramics: lick the suspected area, and it will feel cold.

- Lladro and Noritake are possible buys for the future because they are 'modern'.

Three vividly coloured, late period Foley-Shelley pieces.

The MacIntyre salad servers in the bowl are particularly rare.

A matching pair of Minton blue and white golfing plates.

A pair of Villeroy Boch ceramics – not the author's favourite colour scheme.

The Cambridge Glass Co.: Began in 1901 in Cambridge, Ohio, and produced golf-motif glass in the 1920s.

De Passe Manufacturing Co.: New York circa 1910s.

Handel: Founded in 1885 by Adolph Eyden and Philip J. Handel; based in Meriden, Connecticut.

Heinrich Hoffman: Czechoslovakian who started firms in Paris and Bohemia around the beginning of the twentieth century. He perfected the technique of pressed and frosted glass with the appearance of cut glass.

Heisey: 1920s.

Keroff: Made glass perfume bottles with brass club heads in a tartan golf bag.

Loetz Glassworks: Austria. Established in 1840, and went on to produce great art nouveau glass that rivalled Tiffany.

Monroe, C. F. (Wave Crest): Founded in 1880 in Meriden, Connecticut.

Mt Washington Glass Works: Founded in 1837 in Boston, but moved to New Bedford, MA, in 1876. The company merged with Pairpoint Manufacturing in 1894, and operated until 1929.

Orrefors: Made a heavy glass octagonal-shaped vase in the 1930s with a panel depicting a lady golfer.

BUYER BEWARE
LOST BALL

With knowledge, collectors get to know how to spot a fake; there are many on the market. Some of these were very cleverly executed and the back marks were successfully imitated, so it takes real experience to know the difference. For example, a couple of years ago there was a series of ceramic items offered on the Internet that all seemed to originate from England. However, all were either shapes that Susie Cooper never manufactured, or carried patterns that were never produced by Susie Cooper. Included was a Susie Cooper golfer jug – but the shape was never used by Susie Cooper, the pattern, a brown transfer of a golfer, was not a Susie Cooper design, and the back mark was incorrect, being smaller than normal and actually too crisp compared with the original.

Steuben Glass Inc.: Corning, New York. A major American glass manufacturer.

Waterford, Ireland: Prolific up-market glass, still in existence.

Winarick, A. R.: USA, *circa* 1920s.

Left: An 1826 Burntsfield Links Golfing Society silver 'Golf Subscription Medal' that was 'Gained by Walter Lothian'.
Right: The 1913 British Ladies Open Championship winner's medal won by Muriel Dodd.

The Queen Adelaide Medal. In 1838 the Dowager Queen Adelaide consented to become the Patroness of the R & A. She presented a gold medal to be worn by the R & A captain on all public occasions. From 1853 onwards, the captain has been awarded the Queen Adelaide Medal for playing a single shot in the challenge for the Silver Club by the act of the driving-in ceremony.

BADGES OF HONOUR

Medals

A medal is a piece of metal usually in the form of a coin that is struck or cast with an inscription to commemorate an event.

The first stroke tournament took place at St Andrews in or around 1759. It is recorded in the R & A's minutes that 'in order to remove all disputes and inconveniences with regard to gaining the Silver Club [first competed for in 1754] ...whoever puts the ball at the fewest strokes over the field, being 22 holes, shall be declared and sustained victor.'

The term 'medal', in the context of a token to be received by a winner, was an innovation of the Society of St Andrews' Golfers in 1770, when a gold medal was played for and was won outright. Up until that time the winner fixed a replica silver golf ball to the silver club, or – as was the case with Musselburgh – a medal bearing the winner's name was affixed to the silver trophy instituted in 1774. In time this format of 'fewest strokes' competition became known as a medal, because the victor won an actual medal to keep as a memento.

During the late eighteenth and throughout periods of the nineteenth century, a golfer would wear the coloured coat or jacket (reds, blues and greens) of the society; it was basically a golfing uniform. When in uniform, everyone who has served in the forces wears their medals with pride. When medals began to be awarded to (or gained by) the winners of stroke play competitions, the winner would have been proud to wear it on his golf jacket and show it off to his fellow members. Medals, both military and for golf, became more and more popular following the period directly after the Battle of Waterloo in 1815.

Behind each golfing medal there is usually a story

waiting to be told; it just needs research and time. Always, though, the medal represents one man's triumph over a fellow opponent, or the whole field of players, or the course itself.

Medals come in all shapes, sizes and materials, from precious metals to base metals. Usually gold is reserved for the winner, silver for the runner-up and bronze for other places.

SOME VERY EARLY GOLF MEDALS

The very serious medal enthusiasts tend to limit their collections to only the hand-made medals associated

ALEXANDER KIRKWOOD & SON

David Kirkwood, golf historian and proprietor of Alexander Kirkwood & Son (medallists) of Edinburgh, told me that originally the winner won a charm (as in charm bracelet) that he would attach to his fob chain. As the winner, he would be beholden to purchase a charm that would be awarded to the next winner. The Kirkwood firm were well known for their medal dies that were made in Edinburgh and sent to various medallists around the country. Eventually they decided to make medals, too. Their earliest medal die dates back to 1827, and they were making golfing buttons in the early 1840s. The Kirkwood firm is steeped in golfing history. They made the first 'royal' medal for the Liverpool Golf Club founded in 1869, and in 1868 they made what is the earliest ladies golf medal for the Westward Ho! and North Devon Ladies Golf Club.

A stunning Clarendon Golf Club medal in silver and gold with crossed 'Far and Sure' clubs and ribbon loop, *circa* 1895.

ABOVE: An 1822 Thistle Golf Club silver Winter Prize Medal won by George Logan, together with his winning score card that recorded the scores for each of the Leith Links ten holes.

RIGHT: A rare early nineteenth-century silver golfing medal with 'The Independent Caledonian Golf Club Instituted 1810' engraved on its reverse with its earliest winners, 'H. D. Inglis 1811, H. D. Inglis 1812, D. Wylie 1813'.

with the earliest Scottish golf courses such as Aberdeen (founded as a society in 1780 and became a golf club in 1815), St Andrews, Musselburgh, and Bruntsfield (there are at least four different spellings of this club; remember the client would have been in the upper classes, and the clerk taking details of the medal and its inscription would most definitely have been of lower class, and probably couldn't spell well); also Kingsbarn, the Royal Perth Golfing Society (founded in 1824, and the first Club to be awarded royal patronage in 1833), and the Thistle Golf

Club, to name just a few. And of course there are long-established English clubs such as Blackheath, Westward Ho! and the Old Manchester Club.

In America, the earliest clubs are basically those that formed the USGA over dinner in New York City in December 1894, with the first National Open Championship in 1895. The founding clubs were St Andrew's (the US club has an apostrophe to distinguish it from the St Andrews in Scotland), Newport Country Club, (where the first championship was played), Shinnecock Hills, the

FAR LEFT: The silver Edinburgh Burgess Golfing Society 'Presented to Walter Lothian Esq. Holder of the Gold Medal 16th April 1831'.
LEFT: The Glensaddell gold medal, 18ct gold, first competed for at North Berwick Golf Club in 1832.
BELOW: A gold 1898 Norfolk County Championship medal made by medallists Vaughton & Sons of Birmingham.

Country Club and Chicago Golf Club. These very early medals are beautifully engraved and designed. An often cited superb example of the medallist's art is the Buccleuch medal of the Royal Perth Golfing Society.

Although the majority of such medals were made in silver, there were actually one or two gold medals. For example, North Berwick (founded in 1832) had at least two such golfing medals, one of which came up for sale in an antiques shop in London. It had exquisite engravings, and after many weeks of negotiation and raising of monies, the medal reverted to its natural home. A while later another gold North Berwick medal surfaced, this one engraved with the names of many of the founding members of the R & A, including Sir Francis Grant. On this occasion North Berwick could not buy the medal and it was exported to the USA, bought by a private collector.

Club medals seldom come on to the market, and when they do, they sell strongly: obviously medal collectors have to face the fact that these clubs often have benefactor members only too willing to buy back the club's lost heritage.

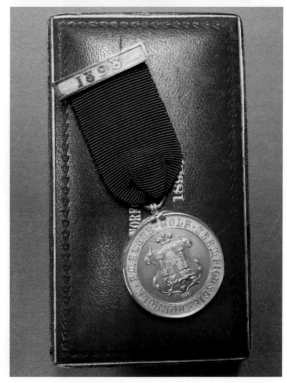

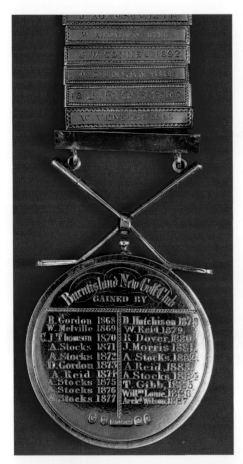

An impressive Burntisland New Golf Club medal first played for in 1868.

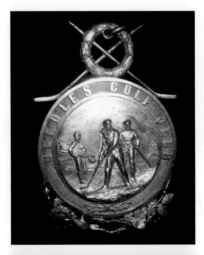

This Needles Golf Club medal measures 4½ x 2in (11 x 5cm).

The Playfairs were one of the very important golfing families at the turn of the century.

Both sides of the early Kingsbarns Bachelors Medal that was first played for in 1840. It sold at auction for £17,000 in 2008.

Left: A large and impressive Heather Club Golf Club 'handicap medal' engraved with its winners from 1906 to 1936.

Centre: A gold King Edward VII challenge medal with an Italianate surround.

Right: The Heather Club Golf Club's 'Henderson medal' with laurel surround, engraved with its winners from 1906 to 1938.

SOME MEDAL TERMS

Brooched: A medal that has been spoilt by being converted into a brooch.

Cast: Technique of forming a medal with molten metal and a mould.

Copy: A replica made to replace a medal that has been stolen or lost.

Cross: Device having four equal arms set at right angles; can be plain or Maltese, with flared sides and double points to the arms, or pattee with flared sides.

Die stamping: The medal was stamped out, rather than being made from a mould.

Device: A symbolic emblem forming part of a design.

Embossed: A raised inscription or design.

Enamelled: Inlaid with a fired, coloured, vitreous coating.

Engraved: An inscription added by hand or machine.

Field: The background area of the flan.

Flan: The disc body of the medal.

Hallmark: The official impressed assay mark denoting silver or gold.

Loop: Ring affixed to the rim for a ribbon.

Medallion: A large medal that was never intended to be worn.

Obverse: The side on display when being worn.

Ornament: Added embellishment.

Relief: A raised design, legend or inscription.

Reverse: The back of the medal, not seen when being worn.

Ribbon: Strip of fabric for suspending the medal.

Rim: When the flan of the medal had been filled up, the winner's names would then go on the rim.

In 1790 the (gold) Medal of the Honourable Company was played for – and it is still played for today. And as then, the winner does not keep the medal, but has his name engraved on to it.

The oldest golf trophy – as opposed to a medal or token that was given to and retained by the winner – is the gold 'Knuckle Club medal' that dates back to 1792. The Knuckle Club members played for it annually. They were Blackheath members until 1825 when the Knuckle Club was disbanded, at which time the medal was transferred to the Blackheath Golf Club. Thereafter it was renamed the 'Blackheath Spring Medal' and played for annually at their spring meeting. Since 1793 all winners' names have been engraved on the gold leaves inside the medal.

In 1774 Thomas McMillan presented the Musselburgh

ABOVE: The large silver Pau Golf Club medal on the left is hall marked Edinburgh 1856 and is inscribed, 'Presented to the Pau Golf Club 1857'; a very early continental golfing medal. The two large medals on the extreme right are silver gilt Derby competition medals for the Berkshire Golf Club played for in the 1930s.

RIGHT: Two beautifully crafted gold Metropolitan Open winner's medals for 1905 and 1909.

Golf Club with a silver cup, to which each year would be attached a silver medal bearing the name of the winner or 'gainer' and the date. Again, although it is a medal, it was not given to the winner to keep.

In 1735, the Society of Golfers at Bruntsfield was formed. In 1800, they became the Edinburgh Burgess Golfing Society. In 1831 the Edinburgh Burgess Golfing Society played for their silver medal of oval lobed form engraved with crossed clubs and golf balls and the Thistle motto, 'Far and Sure'.

The Thistle Golf Club at Leith Links was instituted on 11 March 1815. A very desirable medal would be the 1822 Thistle Golf Club silver Winter Prize Medal that was won by George Logan.

Kingsbarns was formed in the late 1790s. It ceased for a few years, but started again in 1815, then ceased

again in the 1850s, but reformed as the Kingbarns Links, a non-members' Golf Club in 2000. There are three well documented golf medals associated with Kingsbarns. In 1823 they played for the Silver Society medal, and in 1841 the Fielden Medal, both for general competitions. The Fielden Medal features a man with his thumb up to his nose gesticulating in a rather offhand manner; it is engraved with the winners' names between 1841 and 1847, the last a Captain Campbell. The third was the Bachelors Medal of 1840: it was 'Presented by the Bachelors of the Society', and was in the same format and shape as the Fielden Medal, both medals being within a foliate banner. James Naysmith of Edinburgh, who was then one of the country's great medal makers, made it in 1839 to 1840. In 2008 the Bachelors Medal was sold for £17,000 in a Lyon & Turnbull Scottish Silver auction. It was described as measuring just under 3in (7.6cm) in height, including its suspension ring, and weighing 1. 30oz. The nomenclature as a 'gold' medal was only due to its nature as first

Top left: An ornate 15ct Glasgow Golf Club 1912 Tenants Cup medal made by Jason Forest in 1911.
Bottom left: A 9ct Glasgow Golf Club 1928 Gailes Trophy medal made by Robert Scott in 1927.
Centre: A silver gilt R & A William IV golfing medal contested at the autumn meeting.
Top right: A silver gilt Royal North Devon Club medal inscribed as having been won by the great 'H. G. Hutchinson' in 1885.
Centre right: Another Royal North Devon Club medal.
Bottom right: A blue enamel and gold medal for the Portobello Challenge, *circa* 1920s.

prize, and not as the metal of manufacture. There are no solid gold medals recorded for this time, and the laurel leaf border in gilt or gold would have sufficed to denote first place.

The Glasgow Golf Club is the ninth oldest golf club in the world. It owns a silver club trophy dated 1787, and has an impressive silver medal with crossed clubs

ABOVE LEFT: The stunning gold medal gained by the Amateur Champion.
ABOVE RIGHT: The 1874 Open Championship medal won by Mungo Park at Musselburgh.
RIGHT: Henry Cotton had his 1934 and 1937 Open winner's medal converted into a bracelet for his wife 'Toots'.

and ball in gold first played for in 1824; it still features the names and dates of the winners 1825–1830.

Collecting and preserving medals for future generations helps us with the history of the game, with old and extinct golf courses, with players and winners, recorded scores, and names of competitions. Some of the fun of collecting golf medals, especially when there is no clear reference on the medal as to who won it, is the necessary research into who may have been the winner. The same goes when there is a winner but no reference to a club or society. Research, imagination and discovery are essential ingredients to determine the story behind a medal.

A successful research example would be an 'early and important oval-shaped golfing silver medal' that was in a Bonhams auction in 2008. The owner believed it to have been issued by the Burntsfield Links Golfing Society in 1826. The obverse was engraved mainly in capital letters 'Golf Subscription Medal', 'Gained by Walter Lothian Esq Edinburgh'. Unfortunately the reverse of the medal just had three clearly stamped hallmarks, one of which was that of James Nasmyth (J.N.), an active medal maker during the period 1812–1840. The owner, an experienced medal collector, spent hours in public libraries in Edinburgh pouring through 'antiques' books. Imagine his delight when he opened *The Edinburgh Almanack* (also known as the *Universal Scots and Imperial Register*) for 1827 published by Oliver & Boyd of Edinburgh in 1826. There on page 335 were notices on three golf societies/clubs: Burntsfield Links Golfing Society, Edinburgh Burgess Golfing Society and the Thistle Golf Club. Within the Burntsfield notice were details of its council. Walter Lothian was recorded as being an 1826 council member, and more importantly was described as being the 'Medal-Holder'. That was conclusive enough evidence, and greatly enhanced the value of the medal.

Due to the vast number of golfing medals made, some collectors believe it is best to nominate a theme and to stick to it. Themes could include medals associated with the major championships, or with the amateur championships; medals won by specific players; medals associated with a particular golf club; only gold or silver medals; nineteenth- or twentieth-century medals; or specifically female golfing events. In 2008 Bonhams sold the 1913 Ladies Golf Union Championship winner's medal – better known as the Ladies Open before the days of sponsorship deals. Very few Ladies Open medals are known, and this one sold for nearly three times its low estimate, for £8,200 without premiums.

The value of a medal can be determined by several factors, which might include the following:

- the era of the medal;
- the golf club holding the competition (the more prestigious the better);
- the names of the winners, especially if there are some recognizable players;
- the winner's name should be engraved on the medal;
- the type of metal used, with gold being better than silver or a base metal;
- the beauty of the medal, such as its design and mounted filigree;
- long-nose clubs, golf balls and golfers engraved or stamped on the medal will enhance its value;
- quality medals are presented in leather cases;
- whether the medal retains its original ribbon;
- what condition the medal is in, checking for wear and over-cleaning.

The best golf medals should intrinsically be golf in form and design, rather than being just a round medal engraved with golfing details. Some cheaper medals have an enamel centrepiece to reflect it as a golf medal, as opposed to one for cricket or football; this type of medal was produced in its thousands, to be used as monthly medal tokens. These are not valuable, although a golf medal collection should have at least an example of one.

CHAMPIONSHIP MEDALS

Medals from the Amateur Championship are keenly sought. There has only been the one design for this, the oldest Amateur Championship in the world. The design is the same for the gold (22ct) winner's medal, the silver runner's-up medal, and the two bronze semi-finalists' medals. Manufactured by Walker and Hall, it is square and quatrefoil in form, its centre features a late Victorian golfer at the top of his swing, the reverse a laurel garland. Each medal comes with its own box. Of course it is difficult, if the bronze medal is not inscribed, to determine which of the semi-finalists originally won the medal.

Medals awarded to Open Championship winners and runners-up are sought after by medal collectors, Open memorabilia collectors as well as collectors of specific players who may have won the Open. They do occasionally get on to the market. For example, Bobby Locke won the Open four times, and his gold medals

CHAMPIONS' MEDALS

The following champions' medals have come to auction:

1874 Mungo Park (2005) £48,000
1883 Willie Fernie (2008) £48,500
1884 Jack Simpson (1984) £5,500
1885 Robert Martin (1996) £27,000
1887 Willie Park Junior (1988) £13,000
1934 Henry Cotton (1996) £10,000
1937 Henry Cotton (2007) £26,000
1938 R. A. Whitcombe (1989) £9,000
1948 Henry Cotton (1996) £10,000
1949 Bobby Locke (1993) £21,000
1950 Bobby Locke (1993)
1951 Max Faulkner (1995) [estimate £20,000-30,000] failed to sell, with bidding ceasing at £7,500. Now in a private collection.
1952 Bobby Locke (1993) £13,000
1957 Bobby Locke (1993) £19,000

Brian Barnes was a very successful golfer during the 1960s and 1970s, and he was thrilled to win two Senior Open Championships at Royal Portrush in the 1990s where his father-in-law Max Faulkner won the Open in 1951.

MEDAL COLLECTORS' HELPFUL HINTS

- British silver hallmarks denote the sterling standard (.925), the place of assay and date.

- In America, 'top end' medals use 10ct, 14ct gold and .900 fine, and there are no dates to assist dating the medals.

- Go to some of the more established golf clubs and ask to view their medal collections. For example, at Royal Liverpool there are the John Ball and Harold H. Hilton collections; the Four Seasons resort and club at Las Colinas has a great collection of Byron Nelson's medals; the British Golf Museum in St Andrews also has a superb medal collection.

were sold at auction in the mid-1990s. Undoubtedly the centrepiece of any medal collection would be an Open winner's medal!

There are actually two visually different types of

Open Championship medal. The first type was first awarded in 1872: made from silver gilt (silver plated with gold), it was stamped in capital letters 'Golf Champion Trophy'. It was oval in shape, and decorated with a beaded border, it measured 2³⁄₄in (7cm), and it featured a suspension ring to which was fixed a blue ribbon. It was originally boxed. Not all of the early recipients were pleased at receiving the medal; it is well known that when Willie Park Junior won the 1889 Open, he sent the medal back to the Royal and Ancient, saying that, 'If the cheap medal was the best they could do, they had better keep it.' I wonder whether they ever returned it to Willie when he had calmed down? Harold H. Hilton was the last recipient of this type 1 medal; he won the Open in 1892.

The second type of Open medal was awarded from 1893. The first champion to receive the new style of medal was W. Auchterlonie. Made from 18ct gold by Hall & Walker of Sheffield, the new-style medal had 'Open Championship' and the date engraved in gothic-style lettering on its obverse. On the reverse it was engraved 'Winner'. It was round in shape, 1⁵⁄₈in (4cm) in diameter, and it was boxed. Although the above

ABOVE: In 2000, the R & A awarded all surviving Open champions a gold-plated medal redolent of the first type of Open winner's medal.

CENTRE: The first type of US Open winner's medal. Joseph Lloyd was the 1897 US Champion.
RIGHT: This beautiful example of the second type of US Open medal was won by Alex Smith at the Onwentsia Club.

specification is generally correct, in many instances the medals were a little erratic in their thickness and weight, probably a reflection on the cost of bullion.

There are other medals associated with the Open, such as the one awarded to the best amateur who had qualified for the last day; or the Tooting Bec gold medal that is awarded each year to the British PGA member with the lowest score in the British Open.

AMERICAN MEDALS

The US Open winner's medal is another great collectable. There are four different types of US Open winner's medal.

Type 1: First awarded in 1895. Made in gold and decorated with cobalt blue enamel, its scallop shape was fixed to a gold chain with three gold bars. The top bar reads 'Champion' in capital letters; the second bar the date of the Open; and the third bar, the name of the winner. John Frick, medallist jeweller, 8 Liberty Place, New York, made the medal; it measured 5$\frac{1}{8}$in (13cm) and was boxed.

Type 2: A simpler-looking medal that came into being in or around 1903. It was probably 1903 because the Ladies US Open medal changed its form in this year.

Made in 14ct gold, like its British counterpart it became round in form. In relief on the obverse was the United States Golf Association lettering and its impressive bald-headed eagle emblem beneath a beaded roundel of stars; so too was the date of the Open. In other words, it is a one-off medal, totally unique because of the featured date. The reverse was blank to allow individual inscriptions by the winner. It came with a blue ribbon with a clasp, and was boxed.

Type 3: A 14ct gold medal decorated with enamel. The obverse was now in relief with the American bald-headed eagle beneath a beaded roundel of stars on a pale blue background, the eagle superimposed with a cartouche with red and white vertical stripes beneath a blue horizontal band. The capital letters 'Organised 1894' have replaced the date of the Open on the Type 2 medal. The reverse was decorated in relief with a garland of ribbon-tied berried laurel. Measures 1$\frac{3}{4}$in (4.5cm) in diameter, and boxed.

An example of the third type of US Open medal.

The fourth type of US Open winner's medal.

1927 Canadian Open runner's up medal. North American golf medals are keenly sought after.

1926 Canadian Open winner's medal won by MacDonald Smith.

An attractive gold 1911 Memphis Open winner's medal.

WHERE ARE THE US OPEN MEDALS NOW?

- 1895: Horace Rawlings was awarded the winner's medal for the first US Open. In 1993 this medal was offered to the USGA Golf Museum on a loan basis by Michael Rawlings, Horace's great grandson.

- 1896: James Foulis at Shinnecock Hills won the 1896 Open, and this medal is also on display at the USGA Museum.

- 1897: The Open was won by Joseph Lloyd, and this medal was auctioned in the USA in 1990, fetching $21,000.

- 1898: The USGA Museum bought the 1898 medal, won by Fred Herd, at auction for £15,000.

- 1936: The 1936 US Open medal was won by Tony Manero; in 1996 it sold at auction for $23,000.

- 1955: In the playoff for the 1955 US Open, the great Ben Hogan was beaten by Jack Fleck and his winner's medal sold at auction for $36,000.

LEFT: An official USGA 1934 National Open contestant's badge, still complete with a contestant's player number celluloid tag.
BELOW: Very Art Deco in style, and very collectable today.

Type 4: The 14ct gold medal was introduced during the late 1960s; it was devoid of enamel. The obverse was still in relief, featuring the American bald-headed eagle. The word 'Organised' has been deleted. The reverse is decorated in relief with a garland of ribbon-tied berried laurel. It measures 1³⁄₄in (4.5cm) in diameter, and is boxed.

When it began in 1916, the USPGA Championship was a match play event, but due to the pressures exerted by the television companies, it changed to a medal format in 1958. The winner receives a 14ct round medal made by Feue. The obverse is set with a .60ct diamond, and with an inscription in relief capitals: 'The Professional Golfer Association of America Championship' and a panel below inscribed 'Winner' and the date. The reverse features, in relief, a golfer and a mythological winged figure holding a laurel garland over a sacrificial fire. Only one USPGA medal has come

to auction, in 1990, and that belonged to the great Walter Hagen. The USPGA medal measures 1³⁄₄in (4.5cm) in diameter.

Badges

CADDIES' BADGES

By 1910, at many of the up-market American golf clubs the caddies had become more structured and professional. The Caddies' Register contained details of the members and their allocated caddy, who was identified by a numbered metal badge. For example, the American Homestead Country Club provided its caddies with a circular pin badge with an ivorine centre. In Scotland, Musselburgh caddies had an oval brass arm badge with a leather arm strap. Caddies' badges were originally brass- or chrome-plated, later celluloid, and eventually plastic.

COMPETITORS' BADGES

In the Majors and Amateur Championships, each competitor is issued with a player's badge. This acts as an I.D. badge, and gives the player access to the course,

ABOVE: The USGA was far more sophisticated when it came to their badges – this one issued for the 1938 US Open was a real keepsake.
LEFT: Maybe this 1937 Open competitor's badge was Henry Cotton's? We can only dream!

the practice ground and the clubhouse. These badges have become very collectable in recent years, firstly because certain ones will have been worn by the greats of the game, and secondly because they are not badges of honour, they are often discarded and consequently become rare.

In 1910, the USGA started to give their championship contestants attractive metal badges or pins made from yellow or white metal and often decorated with red and white enamels. In most cases these badges were individually numbered so that with a little research the collector today can determine who the actual player was then. Obviously the value of the badge increases with the importance of the player.

Up until 1937, the R & A's competitors' badges were plain card, tie-on badges. However, possibly they felt it was about time their badges were of a comparable standard to their American cousins, and at that year's Open the competitors wore a really sumptuous badge. Unfortunately at this time Britain was in the throes of preparing for war, and although the Open Championship was played in 1939 and 1940, the badges reverted to cardboard. Card continued to be used for the first Open after the war in 1946; rationing and the prioritizing of materials such as metal ensured that the players' badges were at the bottom of any priority list. It was not until the 1963 Open Championship, having been revitalized in 1961 and 1962 by Arnold Palmer, that the R & A issued the competitors with round silver and blue metal badges.

Buttons

Collecting buttons with a golf theme is fun, and visually they make a wonderful display.

Buttons made with an insignia date back to the seventeenth century and owe their origins to the military – and still today British regiments have metal buttons on their service dress jackets, and for non-commissioned officers and commissioned officers, on

BUYER BEWARE

OOPS! THREE PUTTS

Faked golf medals have occasionally found their way on to the market. There are several examples of medals with incorrect hallmarks or 'new' engravings, which appear to alter the age of the medal, and its desirability.

ABOVE: The Open player's badge on the left is an early example.
LEFT: Card badges for the Open are keenly sought-after mementos.

Golfing buttons straight from the manufacturer.

their mess kits. They were – and still are – important articles of dress ornament, and help maintain an esprit de corps as well as aiding identification. As we have read elsewhere, golfers in the nineteenth century wore long-tailed coats or jackets when playing golf. For example, at Crail the jackets were blue, and their golfing buttons set off the outfit. Large buttons were used to fasten the coat, and smaller matching buttons were stitched on to the cuffs.

Golf buttons are usually a one-piece construction, and various materials have been used, including solid gold, sterling silver, fused plate, tin, brass, gilt with centres formed by ivorine discs, and glass tops with Bakelite backs. Such buttons were made in sets, although often only single examples remain.

There are mainly two groups of buttons: the first would embrace buttons made specifically for a golf club, showing a recognizable emblem or letters. Sometimes the name of the club is easily identified, at other times it is only the initials, just like spoons. In the same way as medal collectors, button collectors can collect buttons associated with the earliest golf clubs. A club button would only change when, for example, the club gained royal patronage or merged with another club. Thus a collector would be more excited to find a brass blazer button for Aberdeen Golf Club, than one for the Royal Aberdeen Golf Club. The second group would embrace a general button with a generic golfing emblem; it would adorn a blazer, for example.

A TRUE STORY: OPEN PLAYER'S BADGE

In 1999, the author was helping his daughter Rachel run a stall at her school fair. He had had a good clear out of household rubbish, and their table generated some monies for the school. After three hours he took a walk around, looking at what everyone else had to sell; soon he was rummaging through a wooden box of metal knick-knacks. The stallholder was not a parent but a market trader, so he must have known what was in the box! And lo and behold, lurking in the bottom of it was a little treasure: a 1989 Open player's blue and chrome badge! The dealer wanted £8 for it, but instead he was offered a broken lawn mower – and the exchange was accepted! The author felt like a young Jack (of Beanstalk fame) who had sold his cow and returned home to his mother with beans rather than money!

But two months later he entered the badge in the Philips' summer golf sale where it fetched £230! So yes, there are still bargains to be found, just keep looking.

THE GOLF LINKS & LIFE BOAT HOUSE, BRANCASTER.

Sometimes golf postcards have different collecting themes on them – this one, *circa* 1905, of Brancaster, Norfolk, shows the lifeboat house as well.

A hidden gem – if only we knew where it was. Obviously Scottish, and moorland. Could it be Ranfurly at Bridge of Weir?

MINIATURE IMAGES

Postcards

Collecting golfing postcards remains a strong part of the hobby. They are a pictorial time capsule preserving for ever golf courses as they once were – courses that have long since closed. They provide a social insight into golfing fashions, and the transportation used to get to and from the golf course.

The first postcards originated in 1869 in Austria, and by the 1890s had become generally available throughout mainland Europe. Picture postcards were officially approved in the UK in 1884, and sending postcards became a popular and novel form of communication: it was an immediate success for both the consumer and the relevant postal authority because it was an inexpensive way to send a written message. In time, printers began publishing cards that were suitable for posting, and these featured a pre-printed message or illustration. To begin with these were often actual photographic prints, but they were soon joined by colourful illustrations of golf courses and players. Also, the postcard was originally designed so that the address went on the back and the message on the other, the picture side. Then in 1902 British cards were designed so they could have a written message and the address on the back of the card, and the image on the other; this format was adopted in the USA in 1907. These differing formats can be helpful when trying to date a non-franked postcard.

By 1910 the postcard phenomenon was at its zenith, as was demonstrated by the fact that the British Post Office alone was handling an average of 16 million postcards each week. One contributory factor to their popularity was that postage was cheaper than it was for letters – and of course there were no phones at this time!

COLLECTING THEMES

Popular collecting themes today might include the following:

Famous players from bygone eras: Such as Tom Morris, especially where they are playing golf and with views of golf courses that have held the Majors.

Comic and cartoon-type cards: Especially the saucy ones with lewd jokes, similar to the risqué seaside humorous cards that were sold throughout Britain in resort souvenir shops. In most cases the player finds more than just his golf ball behind a gorse bush! I still have a chuckle when I read the punch line, although it would seem that political correctness has long since forced these 'sexist' postcards off the British High Street.

Advertising: For example, the North British Rubber Company of Edinburgh issued a number of postcards in 1913 to advertise their 'Chick' family of golf balls. The

POSTCARD TERMS

Divided back: Post 1902: cards could have a written message on one half of the back of the card and the address on the other, and the image on the front of the card.

Spoiled: When the sender has written over the image.

Undivided back: Pre 1902: the message is on the same side as the picture, the back being reserved for the address and stamp.

Write-away: A reprinted vignette and words, to which the sender could add a message.

W. B. Torrance, centre with caddy, on a 1922 postcard, most likely a private snapshot taken at Braid Hills, Edinburgh. Are the schoolchildren in the uniform of Torrance's old school, George Watson's College?

Beautiful ladies of the time.

cards have humorous aspects of the rules of golf, and give advice to players. Each has a yellow chick atop a golf ball in the bottom left- or right-hand corner. The legend on the back of the card reads 'Printed and published by the North British Rubber Co. Ltd, Castle Mills, Edinburgh. Makers of the Famous "Chick", "Big Chick", "Clincher", "Diamond Chick", "New Hawk" and "Osprey" golf balls.' In the space outlined for the postage stamp is the chick and ball logo but with 'Play the Chick Golf Ball' imprinted on the ball. Naturally these are popular with golf ball collectors.

Golf courses (topographical): The courses may be long since closed or moved; maybe the greens are actually browns; well known hazards such as bunkers and

TELLING THE OLD 'OLED STORY !

LEFT: Mabel Lucie Attwell was one of the most famous postcard illustrators, designing over 1,500 different postcards, with every theme imaginable, including golf. BELOW: A postcard, published by Raphael Tuck, illustrated by Lance Thackeray and printed *circa* 1904.

THE GAME OF GOLF.
A Difficult Ball.

water features may have altered. It can be fun to see how clever the postcard makers were, and to what lengths they would go to keep costs down. For example, it is not unknown to find two different golf course scenes but with exactly the same players – they have been superimposed on to several holes.

Today, golf ball divers use these topographical golf postcards to identify old water hazards that no longer exist on the golf course.

Club houses: Some collectors like to trace the development of the club house over the years, sometimes from wooden sheds, sometimes cottages and sometimes virtual palaces.

Famous courses: For example, St Andrews: post-

17TH. TEE, ST. ANDREWS   (12)

LEFT: St Andrews is considered by many to be the home of golf, but postcards of individual holes are uncommon. This, the 17th tee, dates from *circa* 1955.
BELOW RIGHT: The postcard on the right is cute, but not politically correct today.

8036 "GOLFERINO."   COPYRIGHT, 1906, BY DETROIT PUBLISHING CO.

COLLECTORS' HELPFUL HINTS

- Postcards are popular with collectors because they take up little storage space; they can be framed and easily displayed; and generally, they are not costly.

- Some early postcards suffer from foxing, or have been 'vandalized' by having the stamp removed. As to condition, clean and crisp cards are the optimum. Things to be avoided if possible are dog-eared corners, and tears and stains to the image side of the card. In the absence of any choice it may be necessary to buy a card with some condition issues: interest or rarity should override condition. However, the price should reflect any damage.

- Are the postcards part of a set of four or six? For example, maybe two cards look the same at first glance, but upon closer inspection, are there differences?

- Postcards are 'cancelled', meaning they are replaced, and hence get the chance to become rare. As with all collectables, it is an irony that the poor sellers are the ones that become valuable, because once withdrawn they would be pulped. The popular ones would sell and sell. Some printings will contain the artist's signature, others will not; the text may be located in different places on the card: the collector has to decide just how many variations he wants.

- Storage: a balance must be struck between keeping cards in a safe environment, and being able to access and view them easily. The accepted modern way is to keep the cards in transparent pages stored within loose leaf binders, when the whole card can be viewed both back and front. But a word of warning: the pages of cheap albums often contain harmful plasticizer that can erode certain types of card.

- Postcard fairs and shows are the best way to search out that elusive card. Dealers will have their stock systematically categorized, so ask for golf or sports and enjoy the search.

- Some collectors only want postcards in mint unused condition, whereas others will only collect ones that have gone through the mail, and still have the original stamp: these are often the most interesting because they may have a poignant message and the posting date can help date the card. A used postcard does not have to be in mint condition as long as it is not creased, torn or dog-eared.

- Recommended reading: Tom Serpell's *Golf on Old Picture Postcards*.

cards will show images of the course with each green and bunker marked, and the distances indicated. Compare the course as it was in 1910 with what it looks like today! Look at how the club house has subtly changed, or how the Old Grey Town itself has expanded. Sometimes this genre of card will feature famous players. Often the card producers came up with an innovative package, such as booklets of postcards that made a great souvenir gift, or as a bulk package, a cheaper way to buy them.

By countries: The British Isles, or by its individual countries, especially Scotland; the USA, and then specializing in courses or players associated with individual states; continental Europe and its individual countries.

The collectable Singhalese caddie postcard, c. 1903.

LEFT: A selection of early twentieth-century postcards.
OPPOSITE: A selection of mainly comical and saucy postcards.

Famous golf matches: Postcards showing famous players such as Vardon and Braid in representative matches; for example in 1905, Scotland versus England.

Golf instruction: The swing, the grip and the putt.

Ladies' golf: Famous players such as Joyce Wethered and Glenna Collett Vare who dominated the game in the 1920s; also the fashions adopted by the ladies.

Caddies: Including the indigenous peoples of Zululand carrying clubs to youngsters playing golf.

Railways and their hotels: These institutions would publish postcards of their stations and associated hotels, and invariably there would be a golf course in the photograph: for example, the Great North of Scotland Railway that in 1909 published several cards featuring the Cruden Bay Tournament with players such as Braid, Taylor and Herd.

ILLUSTRATORS AND ARTISTS

The more famous illustrators and sought-after artists include Martin Anderson (pen-name Cynicus), Mabel Lucie Attwell, C. E. Brock, Tom Browne, Fred Buchanan, F. Earl Christy, L. Cock, Harold Copping, H. Cowham, Charles Crombie, Harrison Fisher, E. G. Fuller, J. M. Hamilton, John Hassal, Holland, Martin, Phil May, G. E. Shepherd, Lance Thackeray (Game of Golf), Venner, Louis Wain, David Wilson and Lawson Wood.

POSTCARD PUBLISHERS

The better known postcard publishers include the following:

SIZES AND TERMS

E.	Too big for albums
E. L.	Extra large
F.	Photographic production
L.	Large
M.	Medium
M-B	Multi backed; there are also instances where there are different backs, but not every front can be found with every back
P.	Postcard

- Bamforth (comic)
- Chimers Arts
- Cynicus Publishing Co. (in 1902 published a small selection of cards featuring golfing figures seen elsewhere in his works, all with a typical golf saying, such as 'Keep your eye on the ball'. There is one very rare card entitled 'The Lost Ball' where the image is a photograph rather than an illustration)
- Graham & Henderson
- Illustrated Postcard Co.
- Valentines (entered the postcard market in 1898)
- Enista Hall
- Miller & Lang
- Tuck (Raphael Tuck was a prolific printer of cards aimed especially at the American market, and included series such as 'Golf Hints', 'Write Away', 'Punch – Golfing Jokes' and 'The Game of Golf')
- M. Wane & Co.
- Wimbush (glamour)
- Wrench (depicting famous golfers and personalities playing, such as A. Herd, A. Kirkaldy, B. Sayers, J. Ball, T. Morris, L. Auchterlonie, H. H. Hilton and F. Tait)

OTHER CARDS

These would include, for example, Valentine cards for 14 February. They too were influenced by the growth in popularity of golf in the 1910s and 1920s. Also, greetings cards at the turn of the twentieth century resembled postcards, and were sent to mark Christmas, Easter and birthdays, and as good luck cards.

Often the lyric or message would include a golfing play on words, such as for 'put' where it was replaced by 'putt'. Today, greetings and anniversary cards, such as may be issued for Father's Day or birthdays, are as popular as ever.

BUYER BEWARE

Reproduced cards have been seen with a genuine postmark. The fakers take a quality copy of a postcard, then get an old card with a postmark, its picture is removed by cutting, and the new copy is pasted down in its place.

Cigarette Cards

Top left: W. & F. Faulkner, 'Golf Terms'.
Top right: Imperial Tobacco of Canada, 'How to Play Golf'.
Bottom: W. D. & H. O. Wills, 'Famous Golfers'.

One of the most popular segments of golf collecting has been that of ephemera in general and cigarette cards in particular, especially those issued prior to 1940.

Although some of the earliest golf cards were issued with other products, the majority of cards between 1900 and 1940 were issued with cigarette products. Hence, they are referred to as cigarette cards. Cigarettes were originally packed in the same manner as pipe-chewing tobacco: in a fragile packet that was easily crushed. The eventual insertion of a cardboard 'stiffener' led, in turn, to the printing of pictures, information and marketing opportunities on these cardboard cards. These often visual and colourful cards were of an educational benefit – but that was not why they were produced. The smokers and/or their children found it great fun searching for the cards, especially the elusive ones, and completing the set; the more they bought

and smoked, the better the chance of getting that elusive card! Remember these were the days before health warnings! These proved so popular that the majority of the tobacco firms were soon issuing cards. The best-selling subjects were actresses and the military, because the vast majority of smokers were men. Sport was also popular, especially team sports such as football and cricket, whereas golf was very much a minority sport and a game for individuals.

The first complete set of golf cards was issued in 1900 by Cope Brothers & Co., a British tobacco company, and was entitled 'Cope's Golfers'. The colourful set of fifty cards remains the 'crown jewel' of cards and includes the great golfers of the time, such as Old Tom Morris and Harold H. Hilton. Another wonderful group

of cards is the set of eighteen photographic cards as issued by Ogden's with their Guinea Gold Cigarettes at the same time; they feature contemporary golfers as well as several shots of a match played between Harry Vardon and James Braid at Eltham. In the 1920s and 1930s two British tobacco firms, Churchman and Wills, issued golf cards within a non-golfing set, such as the two golf cards within the Churchman's 'Sporting Trophies' set in 1927.

Bernard Darwin wrote much of the text for the 1934 Churchman 'Can You Beat Bogey at St Andrews?' set; there were two separate editions. There were also two editions of the 'Three Jovial Golfers in Search of the Perfect Golf Course', the English set comprising thirty-six cards, whilst the Irish issue had seventy-three.

Some of the Wills sets were noted for their wonderful artwork. Two sets, 'Golfing' (1924) and 'Famous Golfers' (1930), are always admired and coveted. One unusual group of cards was 'Golf Strokes' issued by the Scottish

Top left: W. A. & A. C. Churchman 'Can You Beat Bogey at St Andrews'.
Top right: William Clark & Son 'Sporting Terms'.
Bottom: Cope Brothers 'Golf Strokes'.

firm of John Cotton, comprising fifty cards per set, designed to be held together and then flicked through the fingers to give the impression of an action picture.

Thematic collecting, such as collecting golf cards, affords a contemporary record that traces the development of the game, its players and courses over many decades. Only a relatively small number of golf-related cards are produced. It can be frustrating, too, because occasionally golf cards are within a larger set – for example 'Sports Terms'. Some will want just the golf cards, whilst others will want the entire set.

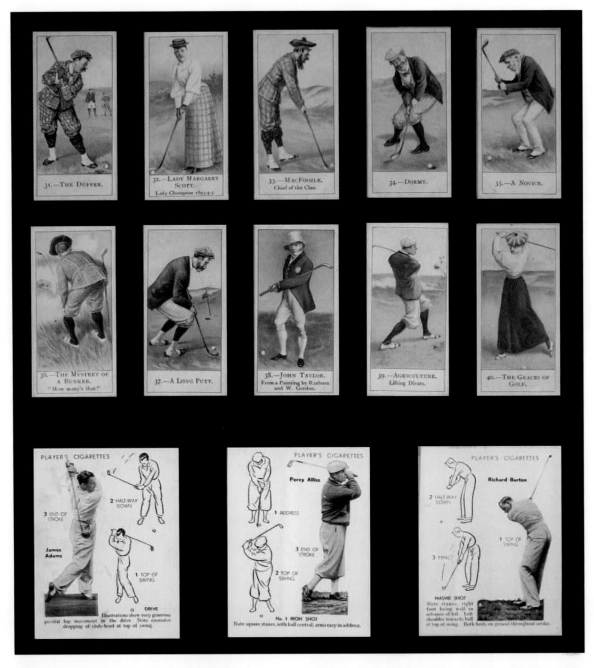

Top: Ten very rare Copes 'Golfer' cards, published in 1900.

Bottom: Three cards from the Players 'Golf' series of 1939.

OPPOSITE PAGE: Twenty Wills 'Golfing' cards, released in 1924.

SOME CIGARETTE CARDS TO COLLECT

Several tobacco companies published golf cigarette cards. Below is a list of the popular British sets:

Felix S. Berlyn

1910 Burline Mixture (Golfers' Blend) Series, twenty-five in the set.

1910 Burline Mixture (Golfers' Blend) Series, twenty-five in the set; P.

Carroll, P. J.

1930s The Irish Open Golf Championship, one card of twenty-four; M (not issued).

Churchman, W. A. & C. A.

1927 Famous Golfers, fifty in the set.

1927 Famous Golfers, A Series, twelve in the set; L.

1927 Sporting Trophies, twenty-five in the set, two of which are golf.

1928 Famous Golfers, 2nd Series, twelve in the set; L.

1928 Men of the Moment in Sport, fifty in the set, ten of which are golf. No. 26 (Walter Hagen) and No. 27 (Bobby Jones) always sell individually with a premium.

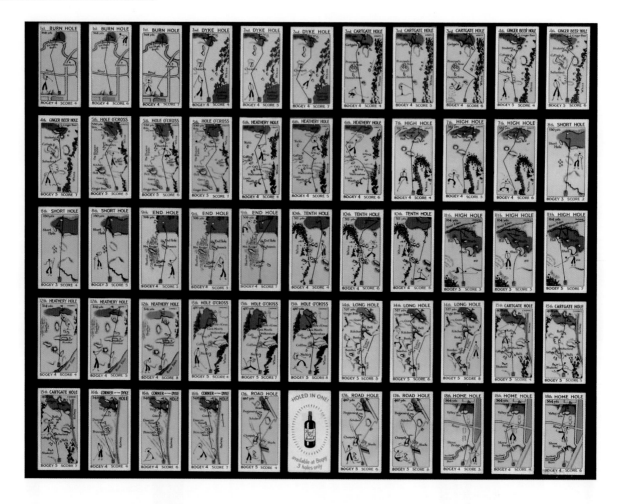

1931 Prominent Golfers, twelve in the set; L.

1931 Prominent Golfers, fifty in the set, coloured caricatures of popular golfers (reprinted in 1989).

1931 Sporting Celebrities, fifty in the set, seven of which are golf.

1934 Three Jovial Golfers in Search of the Perfect Golf Course (English issue), thirty-six in the set. Three golfers, 'Mr Tiger', 'Mr Everyman' and 'Mr Rabbit' play eighteen holes on an inland course, and eighteen on a seaside course; Bernard Darwin selected the holes for Churchman.

1934 Three Jovial Golfers in Search of the Perfect Golf Course (Irish issue), seventy-three in the set.

1934 Can You Beat Bogey at St. Andrews? (1st Edition), fifty-four/fifty-five in the set.

A full set of fifty-five 'Can You Beat Bogey at St. Andrews?'

1934 Can You Beat Bogey at St. Andrews? (red overprint), fifty-four/fifty-five in the set.

W. M. Clarke & Son

1900 Sporting Terms, fifty in the set, twelve of which are golf; M-B.

Cope Bros & Co:

1900 Cope's Golfers, fifty in the set, comprising George Pipeshank watercolours of the leading golfers of that time (reprinted in 1983 as a 'Nostalgia' edition).

1923 Golf Strokes, thirty-two in the set, showing leading golfers executing different golf stokes; M.

Cotton, John

1936 Golf Strokes A/B, fifty in the set.

A rare set of
Marsuma
cigarette cards,
a series of fifty.

1937 Golf Strokes C/D, fifty in the set.

1938 Golf Strokes E/F, fifty in the set.

1939 Golf Strokes G/H, fifty in the set.

1939 Golf Strokes I/J, fifty in the set.

Faulkner, W. & F.

1901 Golf Terms, twelve in the set.

Gallaher

1912 Sports Series,100 in the set, ten of which are of golf showing James Braid.

Marsuma

1914 Famous Golfers and Their Stokes, fifty in the set.

Millhoff, J.

1928 Famous Golfers, twenty-seven in the set, F.

B. Morris & Sons

1923 Golf Strokes Series, twenty-five in the set.

Ogdens

1901 Guinea Gold Photographic Issue: Golf Base I, eighteen in the set; F.

1902 Tabs Type Issue: General Interest Series F, 420 in the set, of which fifteen are golf. The Tom Morris card is mistakenly titled 'J. Morris'.

1927 A.B.C. of Sport, twenty-five in the set, one of which (G) is golf.

1937 Champions of 1936, fifty in the set, three of which are golf.

J. A. Pattreiouex

1935 Sporting Events and Stars, ninety-six in the set, four of which are golf. No. 19 was of Bobby Jones and always sells well individually.

John Player & Sons

1936 Championship Golf Courses, twenty-five in the set; L.

1939 Golf, twenty-five in the set; L.

1939 Overseas Issue: Golf, twenty-five in the set; L.

Wills W. D.& H. O.

1901 Sports of All Nations, fifty in the set, one of which is golf; M-B.

1924 Golfing, twenty-five in the set; L.

1930 Famous Golfers, twenty-five in the set; L.

1937 British Sporting Personalities, forty-eight in the set, four of which are golf; M.

OTHER COUNTRIES

In the USA, 'Findlay Douglas' and 'Alex Smith' (of Carnoustie fame) were two of the six golf cards in a 1910 American tobacco set. These cards are commonly known as the 'Mecca' cards, because "Mecca Cigarettes' were advertised on their backs. Although these six cards are actually a subset within a 153-card set called 'Champion Athletes and Prize Fighter Series', they are generally recognized as being the first 'set' of American golf cards. There are, however, a number of individual American golf cards that pre-date the Mecca set, the earliest by Aug. Beck & Co. in 1883. The Imperial Tobacco Company of

COLLECTORS' HELPFUL HINTS

- Check that the set is complete, that no duplicates have been inserted, and check the condition of the cards.

- Apart from specific golf sets, there are many cards that the collector may obtain from series of a more general nature. Searching through series such as 'British Champions of 1923', 'Sporting Personalities' and 'In the Public Eye' will often yield a proportion of relevant golfing material. It is fun to search in less likely areas; for example, there are two royalty series showing King George VI playing golf.

- As regards storage, you must strike a balance between maintaining cards in a safe environment, and being able to access and view them easily. The modern accepted way is to keep the cards in transparent pages stored within loose leaf binders, when the card can be viewed both back and front. A word of warning: the pages of cheap albums often contain harmful plasticizer that can damage certain cards.

- Another popular storage method is to frame the sets ready for hanging and viewing. Never stick them down; framed and mounted (in America called 'matted') is good, especially so that the reverse of the cards can be seen. Beware of the damage that can be caused by direct sunlight or overhead lighting.

- For more information on cigarette cards in general, contact the Cartophilic Society, which has published several books on the subject.

Canada released 'How to Play Golf' by Arthur Havers in 1925 , and in the following year 'Perils of Early Golf'.

There were several North American tobacco companies who published golf cigarette cards; these are the popular sets:

American Tobacco C. (USA)
1910 'Champion Athletes and Prize Fighter Series',
        153 in the set, six of which are golf; L.
Imperial Tobacco Company of Canada
1925 'How to Play Golf', fifty in the set.
1926 'Perils of Early Golf', six in the set, E.

REPRINTED CARDS
Cigarette card collectors most often choose specific categories and, in the sporting arena, the choice may be made from football, cricket, golf, horse racing and other sports such as billiards and snooker. It could take a lifetime, and great expense to complete a collection. Therefore there has been, and remains, a need for inexpensive reprints to fulfil the collectors' demands. These were never published to be fraudulent, although sadly in the hands of a dishonest dealer and possibly on the Internet, they may be presented as genuine.

OTHER COLLECTABLE CARDS
Other popular card collectables are the cigarette silks that were given away with packets of cigarettes in America during the first couple of decades of the twentieth century. Known as 'college collectors' cards', they depicted golfers dressed in college colours. Examples seen include Brown, Annapolis, Wisconsin and West Point. They measure 5 x 3in (13 x 7.5cm).

Since 1945, golf cards have only been issued spasmodically, and these generally with cigar brands. Other commodities have also issued series of cards in order to promote their product and increase sales, usually tea and bubble gum. General Mills issued 'Wheaties' cards featuring the greats of golf in the 1950s, such as Ben Hogan, Sam Snead and Patty Berg. Such non-tobacco cards are customarily termed 'Trade Cards'. In 1981 and 1982, the American bubble gum company Donruss published their PGA Tour sets of sixty-six cards. These were very popular. Between 1983 and 1990 the PGA Tour continued these cards and they became sought

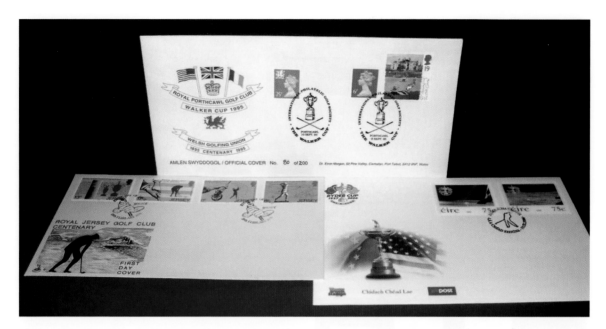

First day covers from Jersey, Wales (Walker Cup 1995) and Ireland (Ryder Cup 2006).

after, especially with autograph collectors, the Holy Grail being a complete set and all signed by the relevant golfers. In 1990 another American company, Pro Set, got the licence to print the cards and three sets were published, in 1991, 1992 and 1993. In the main these cards featured Tour players, but also some from the Seniors Tour. They were all inexpensive, and today may be had for just a few pounds.

Some other modern trade cards are itemized below:

Gameplan Leisure Ltd
1995 Open Champions (Golf), twenty-five in the set; L.
Golf Gifts Ltd
1991 Ryder Cup 1989, twenty-four in the set; M-B.

Ferd, Piatnik & Sons (Austria)
1998 Masters of the Old Course – St Andrews –
        Open Champions, fifty-five in the set; EL.
Sheridan Collectables
1993 The Bobby Jones Story, twelve in the set; EL.
1994 The Golf Adventures of Par Bear, six in the set; L
1994 The Players of the Ryder Cup, 1993, twenty-five
        in the set, EL.
1994 The Tom Morris story, twelve in the set, plus
        two additional substitute cards; EL.
1995 Bobby Jones and St Andrews, twelve in the set
        and one promotional card; EL.
1996 Railway Posters – Golf, seven in the set; L.
1996 Winners of the Ryder Cup 1995, twelve in the
        set; L.

Stamps

Postage stamps with a golfing theme are relatively modern, the first depicting a golfer only released in 1962 by Cape Verde. However, the first golf stamp dates to 1953 with a view of the Unzen Golf course, Japan. Some golf stamps are relatively rare because not

---

BUYER BEWARE

PLAYING OUT OF TURN

State of the art scanners and quality printers are all very affordable and convenient tools for the forger. Fakers and forgers can remove the mention of 'reprint' from the back of the cards and pass them off as originals. Or an image can be copied from catalogues and books, professionally retouched to appear to be the real thing.

Open champions, one and all – issued in Britain in 1994.

many have been made. For example, between 1953 and the beginning of the 1990s, there were just over ninety golf-related stamps issued. Very often it is the smaller, poorer countries – ironically with little connection with golf – that produce the golf stamps, because they are great money-spinners. For example, in 1999 Angola, of all places, issued a set of Ryder Cup stamps featuring players from the winning team!

Stamps with a golfing theme are usually attractive to look at, and can add an extra dimension to a golf collection. Generally speaking there are two main golf stamp categories: firstly, stamps produced whose whole purpose is to mark the anniversary of a famous player or a famous event; and secondly, where the golf aspect of the stamp is rather obscure. The latter category allows for more scope in what is a relatively narrow part of the golf hobby.

The earliest first day cover was issued at the 1968 Carnoustie Open. In fact the Royal Mail set up temporary post offices at the host course so that all out-going mail was suitably franked. First day issues with first day cancellations are desirable.

This continued until 1993. The value of the first day cover was enhanced if it was autographed by some of the competitors, especially the winner.

Normally there were four first day covers because the Open only lasts four days. However, when Doug

Famous players and personalities from the past to include Samuel Ryder, Sandy Herd, Abe Mitchell and Arthur Havers.

SOME PHOTOGRAPHIC TERMS

Albumen: A photographic paper that is treated with egg white (albumen) to enable it to hold light sensitive chemicals.

Blind stamp: An identification mark embossed on to the mount of a photograph, and less frequently on to the photograph itself. The stamp usually indicates the name or address of the photographer or the publisher of his work.

Bromide print: A type of photographic printing paper coated in an emulsion of silver bromide.

Calotype print: The image is produced on sensitive paper instead of a glass negative or film, basically paper negatives made photo-sensitive by salts.

Daguerrotype: An early type of photograph circa 1840–1850s. The daguerreotype (named after one of its inventors, French chemist Louis J. M. Daguerre) was one of the earliest forms of photography. Daguerreotypes involved the direct transfer of the image on to a mirror-like polished surface coated with chemical vapours. This process was significantly quicker than earlier forms of portraiture, and so became widely popular throughout the United States during the mid-nineteenth century.

Gelatin silver print: A black and white photograph printed on paper, coated with an emulsion consisting of gelatin and silver salts. The type of silver salt contained in the gelatin emulsion determined what method of printing was used.

Offset print: A photomechanical print. This is not an original photographic process, but made via transfer of the image from a printing plate to non-photographic paper.

Palladium print: Introduced in 1916 when platinum became expensive and difficult to obtain due to hostilities. No gelatin emulsion was used, and so the final print had a matt surface with a deposit of palladium absorbed slightly into the paper.

Photogravure: The hand-pulled gravure is one of the most beautiful ink processes for reproducing photographs. Gravures were made with a copper plate that often left an indented plate mark around the image. The early hand-pulled gravures reproduced the continuous tone of an original photograph.

Platinum print: This contact printing process was used primarily from 1873–1916, when platinum paper was replaced for the most part by palladium. The platinum print process is extremely permanent and gives rich tones and ranges of greys that are unobtainable in a silver print.

Silver print: A generic term referring to all prints made on paper coated with silver salts. Most contemporary black and white photographs are silver prints.

Vintage/old/modern prints: A photograph printed within a couple of years of the date when the negative was made, is considered a vintage print. Prints made recently from the original negatives are called 'modern prints' or 'later prints'. Most often modern prints are made by the photographer, or made directly under his or her supervision. Modern prints may also be made posthumously and are specifically noted as posthumous prints, often identifying the person who made the photograph.

Saunders missed a three-foot on the 18th that would have won him the 1970 Open, he instead tied with Jack Nicklaus. The play-off took place on Monday 12 July (72/73), and Nicklaus won it. There was a fifth envelope posted on the day of the play-off, and it is relatively rare.

There have been three famous golfers featured on American stamps. The US Postal Services commemorated the 75th anniversary of Francis Ouimet's 1913 US Open triumph with a stamp issued on 23 May 1988.

Earlier in September 1981 Bobby Jones and Babe Zaharias were featured on stamps as part of the American Sports Series.

Other good stamps to look out for include a 1978 issue of a set of four Harry Vardon stamps to mark the 100th anniversary of the Royal Jersey Golf Club. Also, the Alderney Bailiwick of Guernsey in 2001 issued a marvellous set of six stamps tracing the development of golf's implements through the ages: a great set. And Alan Shepherd who took golf to the moon was

A great T. Rodger photograph of the two Tom Morris stars – and it is signed by them, too.

ABOVE: George S. Pietzcker took this photograph of Bobby Jones proudly holding the Havemeyer Trophy.
RIGHT: The Haig ready to fly. At his feet is what is believed to be his 1927 Ryder Cup team captain's golf bag.

Even though this James Patrick photograph of Old Tom Morris is a little faded, its value is enhanced by Tom's signature (£1,000 plus).

honoured in 1972 by a Ras al Khaima stamp issued to celebrate Apollo XIV's safe return from the moon. It shows Shepherd hitting his six iron: the first ball was a shank, and the second went over 200 yards.

There have been several comprehensive golfing stamp and cover collections assembled over the years. The Schulenburg thematic collection of golfing stamps and rare covers from around the world as presented in eleven volumes came to auction in 2001. The covers included the rare and desirable cover dated 13 January 1933 commemorating the opening by Robert T. (Bobby) Jones of the Augusta National Golf Club; a Carnoustie cover signed by Cotton, Hogan and Player; and a block of eight stamps autographed by the subjects of the stamps who were all great champions. Another great stamp collection has been compiled by Dr Gary Wiren.

Photographs

Photographs can be categorized as stills, glass negatives and moving images.

Collectors share the opinion that their photo images bring to life the great golfing moments or the great golfers. Like postcards, they provide us with information on what the players looked like, what the courses were

VINTAGE PHOTOGRAPHERS

- Robert Adamson: 1840s, credited with David Hill for the earliest golf photograph (calotype) of views of St Andrews.

- James Arthur: Active 1890s.

- John Fairweather: Active 1890–1920s. He died in 1904 and his son continued the business. An important image features Andrew Kirkaldy, Old Tom Morris, Ben Sayers, Archie Simpson and Alex Herd on the first tee, St Andrews, in 1895.

- David Hill: 1840s, credited with Robert Adamson for the earliest golf photograph.

- Francis Caird Inglis: Known for the National Tournament St Andrews 1858.

- J. Patrick: Edinburgh based. Known for his shot of Old Tom Morris with an iron, *circa* 1897.

- Thomas Rodger: 1832–1888. Scottish commercial photographer. His images were reproduced from the glass negatives, not as photographs but as engravings. One of his famous images was of Young Tom Morris wearing the Belt in 1870.

- Alfred Hind Robinson: (1864–1950). Known for wonderful panoramic views of golf courses.

- Thompson: Liverpool 1890s.

- R.W. Thrupp: Birmingham active during the 1870s.

- E. R. Yerbury & Sons: Edinburgh, established in 1864.

LEFT: Views of the Liverpool Links at the end of the nineteenth century.
BELOW LEFT: 'This is how you hold the club, madam.'
BELOW RIGHT: Quite a strong left hand.

A rare team photograph from St Andrews in 1897.

like, the fashions of the day and the golfing implements used. Categories could include famous golfers, defunct clubs, trophies, courses, matches and fashions.

STILLS

Glass negatives (half plate) were at the forefront of this new and exciting medium. In 2002 a rare collection of photographic glass-plate negatives sold at auction. They were of an exhibition match of Vardon and Ray *circa* 1900, and are the earliest photographic record of a golf match in America.

Large format, nitrate negative films were popular, and the types of photograph included vintage black and white silver print photographs, gelatin silver prints, and albumen prints.

The earliest known photograph of golf in America was taken around 1881, and shows golfers playing in the area of the original Dorset Field Club. Another photograph taken on 14 November 1888 was of Scott's Pasture, Yonkers, which was to become St Andrew's. Both of these photographs vividly capture the beginning of American golf, as we know it today.

When it comes to values and the collectability of a print, the immediate consideration is to determine whether it is an original photographic print or a later copy. It is a rule of thumb that to be 'vintage' it must have been printed off within a couple of years of it being taken (or within a time period up to approximately eight years for early twentieth-century photos, and within fifteen years of nineteenth-century ones), otherwise it is a 'modern' print (also known as a 'later

Our Captain - M͟r Samuel Ryder - arranged for

1928: A snapshot of what was taking place at this golf exhibition at Stratford.

printing'). However, there are many grey areas. For instance, some late nineteenth-century photographs were printed in the 1920s as prints for 'tourists'. They are quite nice, but they are not vintage, and not modern. These 'grey area' prints can be classified as either 'early prints' or 'mid-vintage prints', or 'printed later'. The latter term is generally used by auction houses to denote prints from old negatives that were made in modern times, usually post 1970s until today.

For a collector there is nothing more frustrating than a photo that has no date, place or photographer, and where the subject matter is not recognizable. Sometimes a little luck is more than helpful. For example, a few years ago, three sepia prints came to auction. The featured hole was the seventeenth at Prestwick, the event was the 1914 Open, the golfer was Harry Vardon, and they had been discovered in the attic of a house in Totteridge, North London, that had been Vardon's home whilst the professional was at South Herts!

The date of a print can usually be determined by the paper used, the quality of the printing, the presence or absence of a signature, an embossed studio stamp on the margin, or a studio rubber stamp on the reverse side of the photo, such as a reference to the Associated

Press and the condition of the paper surface that develops a kind of patina with age.

The pedigree and standing of the photographer is an important consideration too, as is the subject matter, whether player or golf course: the more important the player or course, the more valuable the photograph could be!

BUYER BEWARE

✳ Look for small pinholes, particularly to corners, showing that it may have been on display at some time. Take the photograph out of its frame and check the backing.

✳ With regard to flicker books, beware that there can be missing frames or pages. The staple is more often than not rusty, which has been caused more by the acid in the card rather than damp conditions. Incomplete covers will diminish value too.

George Beldam's magnificent photograph of Harry Vardon.

MOVING IMAGES

One of the earliest cinematographs was made in 1898 at Musselburgh. It features Willie Park and Willie Fernie in a 1½ minute film. Another early cinematograph was made at the Murrayfield Golf Club, Edinburgh, in 1904: it is a 2½ minute film of an exhibition match between the two greats of the time, Harry Vardon and James Braid. There are many examples of aspects of the game that are no longer relevant, such as the golf ball being teed up on top of a pile of sand, and the playing of the dreaded stymie (to block your opponent's line to the hole). Vardon is seen playing his gutty ball (Vardon Flyer) from up against a wall on his way to shooting a course record of sixty-eight. Braid shot a sixty-nine with a Haskell ball.

These pieces of film, quite apart from being possibly the earliest record of golf being seen played, also enable us to view the turn-of-the-century swing in sequence. At that point in time the golfers appear to tee up the golf ball rather further back in the stance than we do today.

The two films discussed above were rediscovered by the owner, who bought them at an auction in the early 1970s with a box of turn of the twentieth-century cameras and equipment. Once the two strips had been identified, it was found that each had been developed on to a cellulose nitrate film that is highly volatile. The National Film Archive, realizing their worth (not neces-

EARLY-MID TWENTIETH-CENTURY PHOTOGRAPHERS

- George Grantham Bain.

- William Barraud: Active in the 1880s and 1890s. Studios in Liverpool and London.

- George W. Beldam: He was a pioneer in high speed shutter photography, and his book, *Golf Faults Illustrated*, was one of the first to publish photographs for instructional purposes, although they weren't much use in reality as the angles from which the photographs were taken, led to misinterpretation. Beldam was the photographer for the famous Vardon sepia image; often these prints bear the signature of Vardon and Beldam in the lower margin of the print.

- Frank Christian.

- Andrew Govan Cowie: (1937–1980).

- George Middlemas Cowie: (1902–1982). The Cowie collection was given to St Andrews University in the early 1980s. It comprises negatives, original prints and an accumulation of old photographic apparatus and old negatives and lantern slides by earlier St Andrews photographers, and also almost 4,000 35mm colour slides of St Andrews by his son, Andrew Govan Cowie. Golf negatives accounted for a quarter of the total to include golf personalities; royalty; Open Championship; Walker Cup; Eden Golf Tournament; golf course views and the Royal & Ancient.

- Georges Pietzcker: Regarded by many as being the top golf photographer in America for the first half of the twentieth century. Pietzcker's work is highly sought after by golf and photography collectors world-wide.

sarily monetary), assisted in the project with their expertise. Both films were copied frame by frame on to a metal master tape.

During the 1920s and 1930s, many of the Opens on

both sides of the Atlantic were captured on film. For example, I have seen a great 8 to 10 minute Kodak 16mm film of the 1935 Open. Exhibition matches too, many with Bobby Jones have been captured on film, one example being a 1922 Pathescope 9.5mm film of a young Bobby Jones, and another a Novagraph 16mm film of Bobby Jones (undated).

In the 1960s and 1970s Shell had the rights to film and distribute many of the classic championships, and these 16mm films were hired for showing to club members. The Piccadilly Matchplay was also captured on film and shown, as was the Masters. Of course there is no need for these any more, with live golf being extensively shown on television, such as the 'Golf Channel'.

MANUALLY OPERATED FILMS

Flicker books gave golfers in the 1920s the opportunity to carry their very own silent movie around with them, and in their own time be able to marvel at and even memorize some of the best golf swings of the time. A series of black-and-white sequential photos were taken of the golfer swinging and playing a shot. These were then printed and bound by a staple to form a booklet. When its pages were 'flicked' like a pack of playing cards, Bobby Jones, for example, began swinging up and then back down again. These books were also known as 'movies' and were marketed as instructional aides… 'Spin the leaves, see the swings in motion'. Measuring the same size as a pack of cards, they were compact and easy to carry in a pocket. Their front covers were often endorsed with sponsors such as Coca-Cola, Abercrombie & Fitch Thornton's of Edinburgh, and Selfridges, to name just a few. In 1928, Schloffer & Wenifch of Czechoslovakia published a Golf Flicker Real Photo Book comprising ninety-five gelatin silver-print photo leaves, featuring an unnamed male golfer. This is a very rare item, and only seldom comes on to the market.

There were three Bobby Jones flicker books: 1A Drive and Mashie; 1B The Rough and Putting and 1C Brassie and Iron. These usually fetch £150 each at auction.

Other great golfers such as Hagen and Sarazen were featured in flicker books, but because of the following, even today, of Bobby Jones, these items do not command such high prices. Sportscope published a series of 'animated instruction' flicker books in the 1930s, and it

A TRUE STORY

In 2004 a couple was browsing the stalls at the Stratford-upon-Avon boot fair/flea market. At one of their stops they spied three large cardboard boxes filled with 'ephemera'. The owner asked £12 for the lot, and the deal was quickly done. Later at home the new owners went through the boxes, reading with interest the letters and looking at the photographs. They originally belonged to the secretary of the Stratford-upon-Avon Golf Club and his two daughters. Sam Ryder had been an important member and had opened the new course in 1928. Amongst the highlights of the contents was 'A Souvenir of a Week-end in the Life of the Lady Captain of the Stratford-on-Avon Golf Club 1929': a photograph album containing over sixty golf photographs, mainly of a thirty-six hole, four ball match played on 14 September 1929 between Mitchell, Havers and two of the Whitcombe brothers for a first prize of £100 put up by Sam Ryder. The first photograph is of 'Our Captain Mr. Samuel Ryder'.

The other photograph album featured a further fifty-nine black-and-white photographs taken at exhibition matches played between 1928 and 1931 to celebrate the opening of the new course at Stratford-on-Avon, featuring such players as Duncan, Herd, Mitchell, Ray, Havers, the Whitcombe brothers, as well as four of Samuel Ryder. The owners brought these and all the other 'bits and pieces' into Bonhams to sell, and in July 2005 they realized nearly £2,000.

included 'The Approach' by Leo Diegel and 'The Long Iron' by Tommy Armour. In the 1960s Peter Alliss and Harry Weetman were featured in flicker books, and these sell for around £40 each.

Another practice aide were the dual-picture cards featuring a golfer and viewed through a stereoscope to give a 3D effect. Examples are fifty Keystone Stereoscope Viewing cards with information on the reverse by Grantland Rice, and thirty Keystone Stereoscope Viewing cards by the Bay State Publishing Co.

This collection of Freddie Tait photographs and letters provides a wonderful
insight to the man and his times.

An Elkington & Co. bronze statuette of
Harry Vardon by Hal Ludlow *circa* 1904, measuring a
magnificent 26in (65cm) high.

METALWARES

This chapter will look at golfing trophies, bronzes and statuettes, and metalware associated with a gentleman, including smoking paraphernalia, ladies' jewellery and tableware, and metal toys.

Golfing Metal Trophies

The silver clubs are the oldest metal trophies, and there are a few examples in some of the old-established golf clubs. It is interesting to note the revival in the interest for new silver clubs as magnificent trophies, with the Scottish medal makers, Alexander Kirkwood & Son of Edinburgh, now making these as special commissions.

Over the years there have been many types of golfing trophy awarded as prizes, and these have come in all sizes and shapes. We have written elsewhere that in fact the earliest golf trophies were ceramics, or even a medal. Since then metal trophies have ranged from silver cups, bowls, plates, jugs, vases and golfers on plinths, with shapes that include two or three handles, goblets and tapered forms.

The joy of collecting trophies is rather like medal

collecting: they are historical capsules that help to maintain for ever the names of golf courses, some long since extinct, and famous international and/or local players and their scores. Often a trophy is named after a famous past player, thus preserving him or her in perpetuity.

At the top of the trophy 'wish list' would be the ones associated with the major championships such as the Open or the Amateur Championship, or with a famous golf club such as Royal St George's or Royal Blackheath.

Wouldn't it be any collector's dream to own the 'Claret Jug'? Though not much chance unless you can win it. In 1927 the R & A decided that the Claret Jug should be 'retired', and that from 1928 onwards the Open Champion would be presented with a full size Claret Jug (known by the R & A as the '1928 trophy') – they would keep it for a year and then return it in time for the next year's championship. This 'second' trophy is identical to the trophy that remains permanently in the R & A building. In 2000, the R. & A. decided to give the Open Champion as part of his winner's package, the medal, the money and a 90 per cent scale replica of the Claret Jug. All pre-2000 winners were permitted to

Left to right: The Edward VIII Gold Cup 1937 trophy, an impressive three-handled silver trophy the Golf Challenge Cup Clarendon Club Manchester 1910, a Vaughton bronze statuette of John Ball, and a modern Swatkins silver-plated half-size claret jug.

Each year the incoming captain would attach a silver (gold if they were royalty) ball to the silver club.

purchase such a replica for each Open they had won. (A similar offer was made to the Amateur Championship winners.) These seldom come on to the market – although there were three included in the Gary Player Collection that was offered for sale as a complete collection in 2004.

When Vijay Singh won the USPGA in 2004 for the second time, as custom dictated he hosted the winner's dinner the following year. For this he had made silver-coloured white metal replicas of the Wanamaker Trophy, each on a plinth and with the name of the recipient and the date of that winner's victory. He gave one to each attendee. A few were also made for attending USPGA officials.

The most valuable and collectable trophies are made from gold or silver, preferably large in size and with intricate golfing decorative designs, rather than just a standard off-the-shelf trophy merely engraved with

SOME GOLFING METALWARE MANUFACTURERS

Asprey: Quality British firm.

Blake, James E.: Founded in 1898 in Massachusetts. Made sterling silver items such as match holders in the 1920s.

Elkington & Co: Famous for its 1904 Hal Ludlow bronze statuette of Harry Vardon.

Garrard: London. Still making high quality items, including the replica Ryder Cup trophy.

Glossoid: Early twentieth century.

Gorham: Founded in Providence, Rhode Island, in the early 1800s. Became the Gorham Manufacturing Co., in 1865. Cast in the 1920s, Sam Bugnatz bronze statuette of Cecil Leitch. Advertised their 'cameras process' that captured an exact likeness that was 'available to your club for a portrait reproduction of any of your champions.' Produced Bobby Jones and Glenna Collett bronze trophies.

Hagenauer, Karl: Austria 1920s.

Heintz Art Metal Shop: Established in Buffalo New York. Made quality trophies and boxes overlaid with silver.

Meriden Silver Plate Co.: Established in 1869 in Meriden, Connecticut.

Nessler, Fishel: New York 1890s to 1930s.

Reed & Barton: Made bronze and pewter trophies in the 1920s.

Samson Mordon: Quality British firm.

Sedlacek: Makers of quality silver items such as cigarette canisters.

Smith Metals Art Co.: Buffalo, New York.

Tiffany & Co.: Founded in 1837 in New York. Still operating.

Unger Bros: Established in 1872 in Newark, New Jersey. Came to prominence during the Art Nouveau period.

Van Riesbeeck: Made plated ware.

Vaugton: Gothic Works, Birmingham. Medals and trophies.

Wallace: Made silver and plated trophies in the 1920s and 1930s.

Walker & Hall: Top quality trophy and medal manufacturers based in Sheffield.

Watrous Manufacturing Co.: Founded in 1896 in Wallingford, Connecticut.

Wilcox International Silver Co: Established in Meriden Connecticut in 1865.

Wood, N.C.: USA, makers of quality pewter trophies.

ABOVE: The Teacher Senior Open Trophy won by Max Faulkner in 1968.

LEFT: Golfing trophies come in all shapes and sizes. This one, the Edward Golf Trophy 1926, is formed by hippopotamus tusks, and doubles up as a time-piece. Not politically correct today, but acceptable in the mid 1920s when it was made. W. Tulloch won it.

the name of the competition and golf club. Other metals or finishes used include gilt, silver plate, copper and pewter.

Golf trophies played for and awarded by golf clubs to their members are keenly sought after. These aren't just bought by collectors, but also by golf clubs wishing to reclaim an aspect of their lost heritage. A good example is the Archerfields Golf Club in Fife that is actively buying back its antiques including trophies that were dispersed when the club ceased to exist.

An immediate consideration would be to determine whether the trophy is the original one played for, or whether it was a full size replica trophy, or a smaller version, to be retained by the winner.

There is a secondary market for old trophies. These are bought, based on their silver content, and can either be melted down for their scrap (based on the current price per ounce) or they can sometimes have the engraved areas polished off so that the trophy is as new. These are often bought in by golf clubs to be used as a trophy for a competition. Cheaper than commissioning from new, intricately designed trophies are still very expensive.

Check that the trophy has retained its original plinth, usually made from ebony, and in later years, bakelite.

These will record winners of the trophy, and obviously the mention of a key player will enhance its value.

'Hole-in-one' trophies are popular collectables. The London-based Silvertown Company, one of the world's most prolific golf ball manufacturers in the 1920s,

COLLECTORS' HELPFUL HINTS

- One frustrating aspect is when the winner's name has not been engraved, as it is usually up the winner to do that before returning the original the following year. A well known exception is witnessing the engraver while the Open winner has not left the 18th green.

- It is easier to date a British silver trophy because unlike its American counterpart there is a date hallmark.

- Always check for clear and well stamped hallmarks, as these date the item and reveal who the maker was. You can buy an English silver hallmarks book for less than £7 on sale in all good high street jewellers.

presented attractive sterling silver golf trophies in the shape of three golf clubs to players who had had a hole in one playing with one of their golf balls. A silver plaque engraved with the name of the player, the hole played, the golf course and the date of the event was attached to one side of the black stand. The other side has another silver plaque giving details of the Silvertown Co. The 1920s and 1930s was a time when such events were celebrated in great style – forget today's paper certificate and hole-in-one tie! The Dunlop Co. issued similar silver trophies.

Bronzes, Statuettes and Figurines

Old golfing 'bronzes' will vary in price from a few pounds to thousands.

The term 'bronze' is a generic term for a dark brown

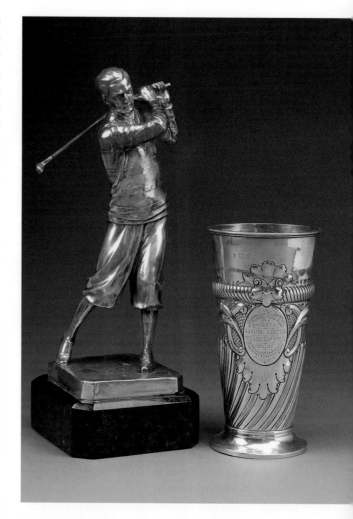

The W. Zwick polished metal golfing figurine, measuring 14in (35cm) high, is thought to have been modelled on Henry Cotton, and was made in the 1930s. The decorative silver trophy is engraved 'Formby Golf Club, 1897, Autumn Meeting 1st Handicap Prize'; it measures 8¼in (21cm) high.

TERMS

Britannia metal: An alloy of tin, copper and regulus of antimony, often mistaken for pewter.

Electro-plating: The technique of applying a thin layer of pure silver to a base metal by electrolysis.

Engraving: One of the oldest of all decorative techniques, achieved by scratching or gouging out the surface with a sharp tool.

Etching: Surface decoration by which the pattern is eaten into the surface of the metal by acid.

German silver: Not silver, but a white alloy of nickel, copper and zinc.

Hallmark: The official marks for signifying that gold or silver is of the required standard of fineness and also from 1784 to 1890 that duty had been paid at the time of the testing.

Silver gilt: Sterling silver, to which a thin layer of gold has been applied.

Sterling: The minimum permitted standard for silver in Britain…925 parts silver per 1000, the remainder usually copper. Also the same standard is used in the USA where hall marking as such does not exist, but 'sterling' or 'sterling silver' is required on all items, meeting the 925/1,000 standard.

metal piece of sculpture or casting; the material used can only be bronze. Bronze is an alloy of copper and tin with some additional trace elements such as antimony, and it has been the favoured medium for small-scale sculpture for many centuries. Reproductions of the original model, itself usually sculpted in clay, are cast from moulds using either a sand cast or lost wax method. Since the late nineteenth century it has been possible to replicate the original in different sizes by a mechanical reduction method, such as the Harry Vardon bronzes discussed later. Moulds, however, wear quite quickly, which is why later numbers in an edition might not be of the standard of the earlier issues – and indeed, many issues of bronzes are not numbered at all, which can lead to poor examples on the market. If an edition is numbered it usually means that the artist has supervised the edition and adds a signature or mark to signify satisfaction with the quality of casting and sharpness of detail.

Another difficult point for new collectors, is that it is possible to make another casting from an existing bronze, and mostly this results in a poor quality figure compared with the original, and also one of slightly differing size. So size does count! An example of this re-casting would be some Zwick figures seen on the market.

Sculptors are usually commissioned by golf clubs to create a statuette that can be used as a presentation piece or as decoration. The most popular medium is either bronze or silver, and such statuettes tend to command the best prices today. Statuettes and figurines can also be made from other metals such as brass, copper, silver, silver plate, base or white metal (in America called 'pot metal'), Britannia metal, spelter, iron and pewter.

The term 'bronzed' conveys the message that the object has been finished with a bronze-coloured finish or dip. Over the years a genuine bronze will develop an appealing sheen or finish, referred to as 'patina', and sometimes this can have a deliberate dark green tint made possible by the addition of verdigris.

Collecting themes include the famous amateur golfers from the late nineteenth and early twentieth centuries such as John Ball. During the 1950s and up to the present time there have been more and more bronzes cast of modern professionals such as Jack Nicklaus and Tiger Woods. These are definitely the collectables of the future.

Considerations include who the sculptor was, and how good he was, and the same can be said of the subject matter. Also, which company cast the piece, and how good was the casting. Bronze and silver are the best metal mediums to enhance value, but this is not the case if in spelter or pewter. Is it an impressive-looking piece?

A classic bronze is the Hal Ludlow statuette of Harry

A Walker & Hall John Ball statuette, *circa* 1900.

Vardon, cast by the Elkington Co. in 1904. There were three sizes: 5in (13cm), 10in (25cm) and 26in (66cm). There are also rare ones made in plaster and a silver-effect alloy material – but even though the former might be rare, they do not have the value of the original bronzes. It is probable that they had been cast from the moulds and therefore lack the sharp detail of the bronzes. In 1904 the 5in statuette was priced at less than one pound (17s 6d), and the very impressive 26in one at £26 5s.

An important question to ask is whether the bronze is an original or a copy. A good example is the Bofil bronze. Spanish artist Antoine Bofil sculpted a bronze of an Edwardian-style golfer at the top of his swing in the 1910s. The original bronze was sold in an American golf auction in 1993, where it fetched $17,500. The vendor had cast thirteen copy bronzes. There was also

SOME SCULPTORS OF GOLF

Bofil, Antoine: Famous for his 1910s bronze statuette of an Edwardian-style golfer.

Bragg, Charles: Made 'The Golfer' in bronze, 1989.

Bugnatz, Sam: Famous for his 1920s bronze statuette of Cecil Leitch.

Cassidy: Famous for his 1901 bronze statuette of Harold H. Hilton.

Codman, E.E.: Modelled the Glenna Collett bronze trophy for Gorham in the 1920s.

Dennard: 1920s.

Faulkner, T.: A Young Tom Morris bronze statuette was cast in 1990 by Alexander Kirkwood Edinburgh; six were made in bronze and one in silver.

Hagenauer, Karl: Austria. Art Deco-style golfing figures *circa* 1920s.

Hassall, John: 1868–1948.

Hudson, G. Petitte: Made a likeness of Jack Nicklaus in 1975 (Selanfer pewter).

Kraczkoivski, Philip: Made in 1972 'The Big Reaping', in pewter.

Lorenzl: Famous for a caddie boy on a granite base, 1930s.

Ludlow, Hal: Famous for his 1904 statuette of Harry Vardon; cast in either bronze, plaster or silver alloy; three sizes.

Gonnilla, G.: Famous for his mid-1890s bronze statuette of John Laidlay; in 1983 approximately

twelve copies were made.

Macleay, Alex: Famous for his 1893 bronze statuette of John Ball; cast in either bronze or iron.

March, Vernon: Harry Vardon bronze.

Mille, Malcolm: Modern.

Parsons, P.: 1950s.

Pearson, Brad: Modern.

Pegram, Henry: Known for his Harry Vardon bronze (11$\frac{1}{2}$in/ 29cm).

Petitto, Alfred: 1980s.

Preiss, 'Fritz' Ferdinand: 1920s to 1943.

Roche, Michael: Made 'Keeper of the Greens', a hand-coloured bronze of Tom Morris in 1991, limited to fifty copies.

Taubman, Frank: Known for his 'Finish of the Swing', *circa* 1895.

Thuss: Known for his bronze of HRH Prince of Wales (Edward).

Tyler, William: Famous for his 1890 bronze statuette of Horace G. Hutchinson (26in/66cm).

Sever, Klara: 1960s.

Spitzmiller, Walt: Modern.

Vannier, P: Known for his No. 7664 gentleman golfer sporting a brimmed hat, 1920s.

Zwick, W: 1920s.

a written guarantee in which it was stated that there would be no more copies cast from that mould. The mould was also part of the lot, and was sold with the original Bofil figurine. These copies can be distinguished from the original at the point where the figure meets the base, where there is a mark basically to say that it is a replica.

The 1920s and 1930s was an era that produced much sporting statuary in small sizes for the modern home. This was also the age of Art Deco, with figures in carved ivory and mixed metals on marble or onyx bases, such as that produced by Ferdinand Preiss. His German factory of Preiss and Kassler made many sporting sculptures in this period, many associated with the Olympic Games of 1936.

Metalware for the Gentlemen

One of the earliest – if not the earliest – silver presentation piece to be associated with the Open Championship purportedly dates back to 1866–7! It was a silver snuff box engraved 'To W. (Willie) Park, on his achievement on winning the Championship at the Prestwick Golf Club, presented by friends & colleagues as a testimony of their esteem 1867', and was presented to him in 1866. Willie Park won the first Open Championship in 1860, and he won it again in 1863, 1866 and also in 1875. Unfortunately, the engraving turned out to be more modern than it looked!

For men there is a great selection of silver and silver-plated desktop pieces, all with a golfing theme, which appeared in the early 1900s, such as inkwells in the shape of guttie golf balls and with crossed clubs. It is often a point of debate whether a golf-club inscription adds to, or detracts from the value, and to an extent it will depend on the importance and significance of the club and player in question.

There is a wide range of golfing metalware to collect. Look out for silver snuff boxes and ink wells some formed by a ram's horn; golfing pens and propelling pencils in the shape of golf clubs; silver-plated car radiator mascots in the shape of a golfer; bookends usually in bronze, each decorated with a golfer and last but not least, pocket watches in the shape of mesh-patterned golf balls. Sometimes these are marked 'Dunlop'.

Smoking and Drinking Paraphernalia

Again, there are plenty of diverse items to collect, such as cigarette cases often with embossed golfing decoration; cigarette boxes in silver and other metals (these are popular today as trinket boxes); ashtrays, often enhanced with an attached golfer or caddy; Vesta cases (also known as a match safe), often decorated with an enamel golfing scene and usually crafted in silver or silver plate.

Cocktail sets were popular in the 1920s, and a popular golfing piece was the shaker in the form of a golf bag with ten or so golf-bag beakers. Whisky flasks, often decorated with golfers, were great for a wee nip at the half-way point of a game!

John Hassall (1868–1948) was one of Britain's best known cartoonists and illustrators during the 1920s and 1930s, and he had a particular liking of golf and its associated personalities. He is credited with what has become known as the 'Hassall Man', an ashtray with a comical-looking golfer. He has a golf ball for his head, and is smartly attired as an Edwardian golfer in an orange-red golfing jacket, with matching hat and gaiters that protect his shoes. Strangely, even though the figure and ashtray were made in the late 1920s, the surface of the head, a simulated golf ball, is of the bramble variety with its pattern of raised pimples resembling a blackberry, and this golf pattern had really gone out of fashion by the 1910s. The head is attached to the body by a rubber thread so that it could

When the Bofil statuette comes to auction it invariably fetches £500.

be easily repositioned, and he is attached to a metal green 'grassy' circular base that has been clearly signed by Hassall.

Most collectable golfing memorabilia categories comprise non-functioning items such as golf clubs, balls, art and ceramics. There are a few exceptions, however, and these include mechanical toys, clocks and watches. Another example would be the Art Deco-style thermometers: a popular one was the Kozy Komfort, measuring 7in (18cm) in height. It was made from a stained white metal and was made in Milwaukee, USA, between 1910 and 1920. The same firm made an extensive range of clocks, and they soon learned that by placing a golfer on top of what in essence is just an ordinary household item, they could sell it for twice the normal price – and sell twice as many, too. They were popular golfing prizes. Often the golfing figure is partially detached due to the softness of the white metal, more often than not the golf club is missing, and the gauge no longer works. Obviously these have an effect on the overall value of the object.

A late Victorian golf presentation table ink stand, its capped double horns united by an electroplated oval mount, surmounted by a cast golfing figure, flanked by a pair of gutty-style golf-ball ink pots. Length 19in (48cm).

An electroplated golf presentation table snuff mull, made by Walker & Hall, dated 1903, the hinged cover with a golfer in full swing as the finial. Length 25in (62cm).

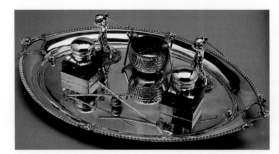

ABOVE: A silver-plated clubhouse ink stand, circa 1900, of oval shape, with a gutty ball-shaped stamp holder, two golfers, two inkwells, crossed clubs and pen rack. 22in (56cm) long.

RIGHT: A fine silver Victorian inkwell made by Elkington & Co, hallmarked Birmingham 1894.

Metalware for the Ladies

For the ladies, items can begin with tableware. Solid silver salt and pepper condiments resembling line-meshed gutty golf balls were fashionable tableware items between the 1880s and 1920s. They were relatively expensive then, so it is likely that golf clubs or societies would have bought them as golfing prizes. The top-of-the-range condiments had the base of each 'ball' flat, obviously to prevent them rolling off the dinner table. When first made they would have been packaged in a leather-clad box, and this would have added to their present-day value.

Although not as popular as it once was, mainly because of the cleaning involved, spoon collecting remains popular with many of the golfing memorabilia fraternity, especially lady collectors. There are many shapes and types to collect. Some have golfers at the top of the spoon in various poses; or the initials of golf clubs; the club's badge or emblem on the top of the spoon; golfers in relief on the bowl; and then there are the many different types of handles and stems, to include spoons with circular finials, decorative embossed shield finials and crossed golf clubs. The ultimate goal is to make up sets of six identical spoons, all having the same silver hallmark. Such sets of spoons were often used by golf clubs in their dinning rooms, or in some instances awarded as prizes instead of medals or replica trophies. One of the most common sets of spoons is the 1930s Churchman (as in tobacco products) Sheffield hallmarked silver spoons with crossed clubs at the top. They were presented in a grey snake-skin-covered case and were used as a promotional gift. They are relatively easy to find.

COLLECTORS' HELPFUL HINTS

- Remember that 'bronzed' doesn't mean bronze!

18
- There are two other important aspects to their collectability and value: is the golfer recognized, and has the piece been signed, dated and numbered by the sculptor?

A rare, cold-painted bronze figure circa 1920, the base stamped 'Austria'.

Sometimes it happens that an item of golf memorabilia will be just as popular, if not more so, with collectors in another hobby. For example, an early George V novelty pincushion or hatpin stand in the form of a robin holding under his wing a silver golf club came to auction in 2005. Levi & Salmon of Birmingham made it in 1910, and there was just as much interest in it from the needlework and tapestry collecting fraternity as the golfers.

Other popular golfing collectables for the ladies, usually in 18ct and/or 9ct gold or sterling silver, could include 1920s silver manicure sets, comprising five pieces each with golf-club tops fitted into a leather miniature bag; Victorian gold and white gold golfing pins and brooches, some with a pearl 'ball'; silver note-cases often with a fitted pencil, the front embossed

FAR LEFT: Look at those curves and the close-fitting clothes! Dressed like that she would have turned many a head at any golf club. Beware, this particular piece has been faked.

LEFT: A Levi & Salmon of Birmingham novelty pincushion or hatpin stand, *circa* 1910.

BELOW: Players' wives and girlfriends would receive such gold charms at the Bob Hope Classic.

with a caddy boy or lady golfer; gold propelling pencils in shape of a golf club; and pillboxes and hatpins in the shape of long-nose golf clubs.

Art Deco lady golfer figurines in the process of completing their swings are popular today. Many of them were sculptured to ooze sex appeal, with a suggestive smile and a rather risqué demeanour. They were made to titillate, and were aimed at a specific market who were not necessarily golfers. However, beware, because there are fakes on the market. Whereas the originals would have been cast in the 1920s, these reproductions were most likely made in the Far East, such as Macau or China. Unlike the polychromed originals that were made from a spelter or pot metal, which is a lighter and cheaper substance than, for instance, bronze, these copies are usually made from resin.

Metalware for Children

There have been a few metal mechanical golf toys made in the 1920s. Ferdinand Strauss, an American toy

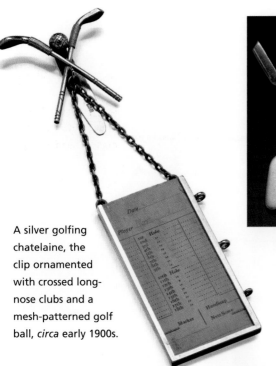

A silver golfing chatelaine, the clip ornamented with crossed long-nose clubs and a mesh-patterned golf ball, *circa* early 1900s.

A late Victorian gold and citrine set brooch with a central 'far and sure' ribbon banner.

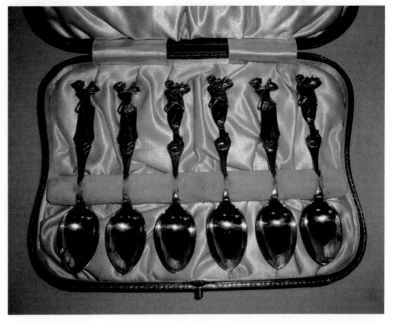

Look at the detail on this Victorian era silver score device.

These beautiful spoons are so eye-catching: three with a lady golfer and three with a male golfer, all six spoons dressed in Edwardian garb.

RIGHT: The highly regarded firm William Mammatt & Son of Sheffield made this condiment set in 1893. The silver-plated ink stand, engraved 'Heinemann Trophy', was made in 1894.

BELOW: The 'UC' Golf Score Recorder, *circa* 1920: one side is made from a mother-of-pearl veneer, the other from a cream-coloured bakelite.

Spoons and vesta cases are often faked, so beware. In the early 1990s a reputable auction house sold a quantity of spoons, some with a male golfer and some with a lady golfer at the end of their handles. Someone had fraudulently (not necessarily the owner) reproduced the top half of the spoon – the male and lady golfer – and then soldered them to a set of bottom half genuine silver spoons with correct assay marks!

One giveaway clue was the slight difference in the silver colour between the top and the bottom of the spoon, and also the fettling between the cutouts around the shoulders was not very clean – it appeared a little rough and unfinished. They were purchased by a group of dealers who then divided them up and the spoons disappeared as genuine into the market. Obviously this practice was illegal.

Some fraudulent people will rub away the hallmarks and substitute them with earlier ones, a practice known as 'rubbing'.

company, made the 'Jocko (Scotland being the home of golf!) the Golfer' toy in or around 1927. The toy was also marketed as 'Play Golf'. It was made from lithographed tinplate to resemble a golf course/green.

Basically, after one player had taken a turn at activating the golfer to stroke the steel ball towards the nine holes at the far end of the 'green', the clockwork mechanism automatically re-teed the ball for the next player to putt it into the hole.

Measuring 12 x 7 x 2½in (30 x 18 x 6cm) and selling for $1, it was described as 'a dandy game' and there was a 'hint to hostesses – give a Play Golf party – it's all the rage'. Some party!

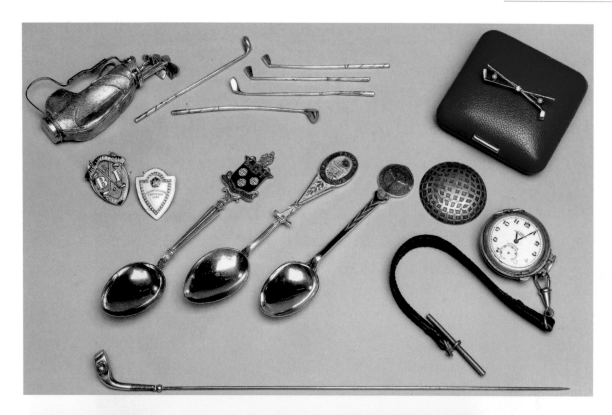

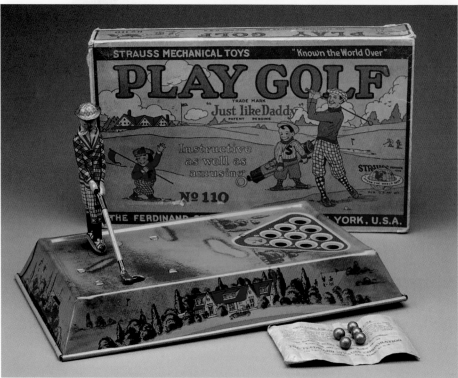

ABOVE: A varied collection of jewellery, badges and silverware.

LEFT: It is amazing that this clockwork toy still has its ball bearing-style golf balls.

Top: The autograph book contains 1933 Ryder Cup team signatures.

Middle left: Shows how the great J. H. Taylor signed.

Middle right: An early Bobby Jones autograph.

Bottom: More 1930s Ryder Cup autographs, including that of Samuel Ryder.

AUTOGRAPHS AND PROGRAMMES

Daily Telegraph, 8 August 2007:

Padraig Harrington (2007 and 2008 Open Champion) confirmed yesterday that he had ordered 1,000 copies of the 18th-hole flag from Carnoustie, along with three replicas of the Claret Jug at a cost of around £70,000. Harrington had asked other major winners what championship memorabilia they had needed, and someone had said they had purchased 500 flags and it had been far too few ... signed flags are apparently the answer for charity auctions.

Autographs

Collecting the signatures of famous sportsmen, celebrities, politicians, artists and film stars has been a popular hobby or pastime for many hundreds of years. Golf is a relative newcomer in terms of collecting signatures of famous golfers, some of whom may have been famous in the nineteenth century.

There is much fun and satisfaction from the pursuit and successful acquisition of a signature of a famous golfer. The fun is in the chase! People who collect golf autographs in person, by standing behind the 18th green or on the pathway to the practice ground at the Open, feel an empathy towards the signer, because there may have been eye contact, maybe even a few words from their hero such as 'This pen isn't working' – 'Who shall I dedicate it to? – even 'Do you know who I am?'

Another important aspect of collecting autographs is owning or holding a letter written by a famous golfing hero. Not only does the letter offer the reader an instant snapshot of the writer's life, it is also personalized by the signature.

For serious historical collectors, a 'must have' set of autographs would be those of the 'Great Triumvirate', Britain's three best professionals in the pre-war era: Harry Vardon, J. H. Taylor and James Braid. The print showing the three great golfers is seen in many club houses. John Henry Taylor is closely associated with both Westward Ho! and his club-making firm Cann & Taylor, and of course the Professional Golfers' Association. James Braid was a wonderful golf

Shoes, gloves, visors can all be autographed and make an unusual display point.

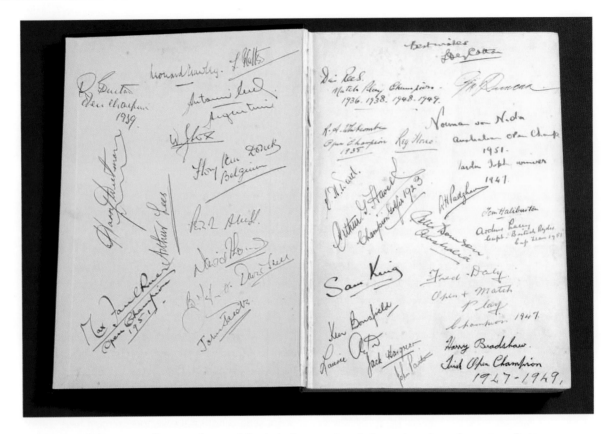

architect, and there are collectors who specialize in just the golf clubs he is associated with. He was the first professional at Walton Heath, 1904 to 1950, and there have only been two professionals at the club since. Although the signatures are only facsimiles, there is at least one in existence with real signatures.

Here are some classic autograph examples:

J.H. Taylor

James Braid

ABOVE: Autographs galore...how many Open Champions can you count?

Tom Morris

Harry Vardon

The 1960s equivalent triumvirate would be Arnold Palmer, Jack Nicklaus and Gary Player, and for the early twenty-first century it would be Tiger Woods, Phil Mickelson and probably Ernie Els!

Many movie 'buffs' and golfers will have seen Ben

Mr Hogan's 1-iron shot to the 18th green, during the final round of the 1950 US Open at Merion.

Hogan's life story *Follow the Sun*, and there is an attractive film poster starring Glenn Ford and Anne Baxter who played Ben and Valerie Hogan. Hogan signed a few of these posters, probably as items to promote the film, and these are very desirable. The same cannot be said of the Spalding black and white promotional poster showing Hogan hitting a long iron on the way to winning the 1950 US Open at Merion Golf Club. These posters feature a very clear Hogan signature at lower right, but they are all facsimiles. The Hogan signature is meticulous, crafted in beautiful script letters, and it certainly enhances a picture, poster or programme. Ben Hogan's swing was captured for posterity in a Magic Eye movie flicker book entitled the *Smashing Drive*, and these are very collectable, as are signed copies of his classic instructional book, *Five Lessons: The Modern Fundamentals of Golf* first published in 1957.

Another popular collecting theme is collecting the autographs of all surviving Open or Masters Champions, or Ryder Cup captains and Ryder Cup players. There is something very satisfying in getting the autograph of a

Ben Hogan's signature (bottom right) was printed on to the poster.

A TRUE STORY

A really serious collector of programmes once in a while wanted Mr Hogan's autograph to grace the programme, menu or photograph. Knowing how busy he would be, this collector decided not to write directly to Mr Hogan at his Texas headquarters with requests for him to sign items; instead he found out who was Mr Hogan's secretary (and letter opener), successfully made contact with her, and made sure that each Christmas she received a great present. This arrangement continued for years, and she would take his item to Mr Hogan who never refused her request to sign...

ABOVE: This Jack Nicklaus £5 note comes with an excellent provenance.

RIGHT: Jack Nicklaus signed this wonderful Craig Campbell painting of himself waving his farewells at his last Open in 2005, and it was mounted and framed with a signed £5 note.

young hopeful amateur before he goes on to become a Majors winner! For example Ulsterman Rory McIroy, who did so well as an amateur in the 2007 Open, is surely destined to win a Major as a professional…

In 1996 Sotheby's auctioned the Henry Cotton archive, comprising the majority of his extensive golfing estate, medals, clubs, photographs, personal scrapbooks, handwritten articles, handwritten and signed letters, and congratulatory telegrams from friends and admirers for his three Open wins. This infusion of

treasured artefacts was literally devoured by collectors keen to own a piece of Cotton's history. Cotton, like Vardon, took great care when writing his signature; it was distinctive and neat. However, because (Sir) Henry was such a prolific signer, his autograph today is not very commercial; indeed it must rank as being one of the most common autographs of a famous golfer.

With autographs the quality of the penmanship is paramount. Consequently the signature should preferably be in black or dark blue ink (an exception would be

Darren Clark who favours 'Irish green' ink); it should be clear, bold, clean and smudge free, and there should be a good contrast between the colour of the signature and its background. One problem with today's modern 'blue' Open programmes is that the covers are laminated and only felt-tip pens show up well. Maybe it is a case of the R & A introducing this type of cover material to deter autograph hunters chasing the players!

There is something wonderful about a well presented autograph, when obviously the signer had taken his or her time over it. The difficulty comes when a player has to sign quickly in an attempt to satisfy all the autograph hunters...more often than not the signature is barely recognizable and really of not much use.

Today, Tiger Woods when signing items – for example, at the bequest of his management team – has a good, clear, uniform signature. However, more and more do we hear of signatures being produced by computers and laser pens.

When looking at a signature, take the time to check that, for example, the letters in a dedication are not touching any part of the autograph. If so, this will make it difficult to cut and mount the autograph within a framed montage of the player, and so will be less valuable, especially to dealers.

How can we know if the autograph is authentic? Obviously a collector can vouch for the ones that were obtained in person. Good sources for autographs include reputable dealers, auction houses and experienced collectors who would be prepared to back the genuineness of the signature with a guarantee.

During the 2006 Open at Royal Liverpool, every competitor was asked to sign the mount of a limited edition print. In fact there were two prints, and both were signed. They are different because some of the signatures were in different positions on the mount. A space was left for the 2006 Open Champion to sign after the event, and it was lucky Royal Liverpool, because as Tiger Woods was the 'Champion Golfer', he signed it twice.

Autograph collectors tend to seek signed items such as photographs, programmes with a signature on the player's profile photograph within, posters, letters, postcards, signed books or souvenir 18th-hole flags.

Golf balls often prove unpopular items to sign because of the dimples and the uneven surface. In fact

One of the earliest surviving Open Championship draw sheets; this one dates to 1899.

some modern players refuse to sign golf balls because a faked autographed ball can be passed off as being just a badly signed golf ball, with the story that the player was signing the ball as he walked! Ironically, however, those that do sign have to concentrate more than normal, and often the end result is very good. Some are very valuable, too. An autographed Spalding golf ball used by Robert Jones when he won the 1930 Open sold at auction in 2003 for £5,000.

COLLECTORS' HELPFUL HINTS

Faded signatures and touching letters should be discounted.

Programmes

Golf programmes are great fonts of knowledge, especially those containing players' profiles, course layouts and hole-by-hole descriptions. They also provide snapshots of what was happening in golf at that time, with contemporary advertisements, statistics and photographs. Programmes from all the major championships are very collectable, including the Ryder Cup, Walker Cup and both Amateur Championships. At the other end of the scale are non-Major events, such as PGA Tour programmes; these have limited appeal. By their nature the majority of programmes are discarded after the event, and so surviving examples become rare.

The oldest Open programme dates from 1921 when the Championship was played at St Andrews. It is much sought after, with probably fewer than ten survivors, so it is extremely rare, and its demand has been enhanced because this was the first Open played by a young Robert T. Jones. These early programmes were unofficial, printed locally, with all proceeds going to local charities. It wasn't until 1927, at St Andrews, that the 'Royal and Ancient' crest first appeared on an official publication.

The covers of the early Open programmes were quite similar, differing only in colour. For instance at the 1936

Open, the final day was a Saturday rather than the usual Friday, and so some programmes can be found with the Friday day and date blacked out, and replaced with the Saturday. This came about because the Monday qualifying round was a washout due to the weather, and was scrubbed. The 1938 and 1939 'programmes' were little more than draw sheets just detailing the pairings listings. Remember war was soon to be

Carnoustie hosted the Open Championship in 1931, 1937, 1953, 1968 and 1975. There was then a lengthy wait until it returned in 1999.

a reality, and paper material had already been earmarked as a precious commodity.

Until 1965, the Open had its qualifying rounds on the Monday and Tuesday of Championship week, with the Championship proper starting on the Wednesday and then concluding with the final thirty-six holes being played on the Friday; this was because in those days the vast majority of competitors were British club professionals who had shops to open and members to serve over the weekend. In 1966 the Open was for the first time played over four consecutive days of eighteen holes with fifty-five competitors playing on the last day, a Saturday. This change brought larger gate receipts and allowed television broadcasting to a much greater audience. The format was changed again in 1980 to allow a Sunday finish.

As in all collecting, condition is paramount, because the natural elements can be an important factor in making some programmes more collectable than others – the survival rate of the programmes could be affected by how wet the days of play were, and usually these soggy pieces of paper would be discarded in the bins by the exit points. Both the 1960 and 1961 Opens famously suffered inclement weather, which has added scarcity value to programmes from each of these years.

Also, has the programme retained its order of play vouchers, order of play draw sheets, and its admission badges (those used by members of the R & A always sell with a small 'snob' premium)? Some collectors don't like their programmes with the scores written in, others feel it is a benefit and adds to the 'provenance'.

A great set of programmes is for the 1930 Open, the US Open and the two Amateur Championships. Of course 1930 was the memorable year, in which Robert T. Jones won the Grand Slam of the four available Majors all in the one year. Being an amateur golfer, Bobby Jones' Grand Slam comprised four events: the US Amateur, the US Open, the British Amateur and the Open Championship. This was a time when his two main rivals, Walter Hagen and Gene Sarazen, who were then the greatest professional golfers, only had three professional events (the Professional Golfers' Association of America Championship started in 1916) in their Grand Slam. Bobby Jones as an amateur couldn't play in the PGA Championship, and it wasn't until the 1930s that Jones' own Masters Tournament was

BUYER BEWARE

OUT OF BOUNDS

* Autographs on visors and used or new golf gloves are not so valuable.
* Obviously keep the autographs out of direct sunlight.

LEFT: The 1930 US Open programme is the Holy Grail of all golf programmes, mainly because of the Bobby Jones connection.

ABOVE: In 1948 Britain's economy didn't enable the R & A to produce a substantial programme.

A fine selection of Open programmes between the late 1950s up to 1967.

recognized as the fourth 'modern' major. With the passage of time, the two national Amateur Championships lost some of their significance and were then no longer regarded as being part of any modern Grand Slam.

In that magic year 1930, Jones won the Amateur at St Andrews. Two weeks later he won the Open at Royal Liverpool. The third leg of the Grand Slam was at Interlachen Country Club in Minneapolis, where he won the US Open after shooting a great sixty-eight in the third round. There was a long wait until the US Amateur took place at the Merion Cricket Club (East Course), Ardmore, Pennsylvania between 22 and 27 September. Jones was the leading stroke-play qualifier, and in the match-play final he beat Eugene Homans eight and seven.

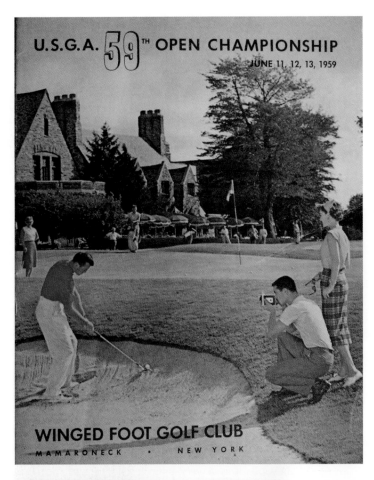

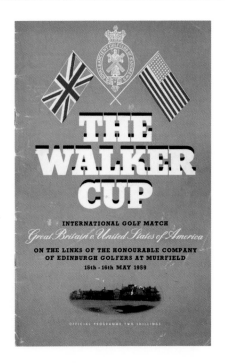

LEFT: The 1959 US Open took place at the famous Winged Foot Golf Club.
ABOVE: The seventeenth Walker Cup 'International Golf Match' took place at Muirfield in 1959.

LEFT: The value of this 1951 Open programme has been doubled with this array of players' autographs including the winner, Max Faulkner.
FAR LEFT: A selection of collectable Ryder Cup and Open Championship programmes.

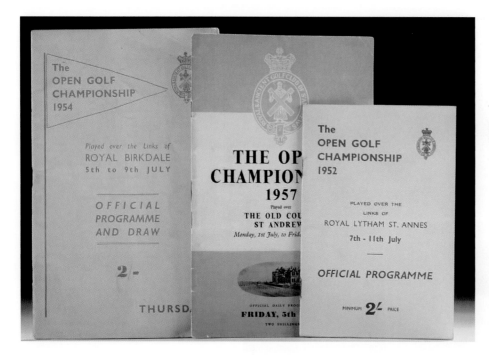

Three good Open programmes: 1954, 1957 and 1952.

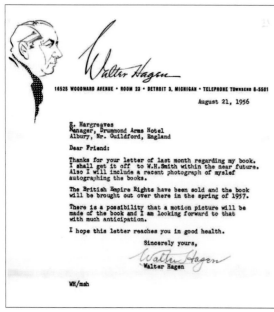

Looks the real thing, doesn't it? But it was probably signed for Hagen by a secretary because he had so many letters to reply to.

The question is, will the four programmes for the Majors associated with Tiger Wood's Slam – his four wins in a twelve-month period but not in the same year (2000 and 2001) – be sought after in years to come?

The oldest USGA Open Championship programme dates back to 1923 when the US Open was played at Inwood. It is a very difficult one to find, not only because of its age, but also because this was Robert T. Jones' first Major.

The 1951 programme is one of the most desirable

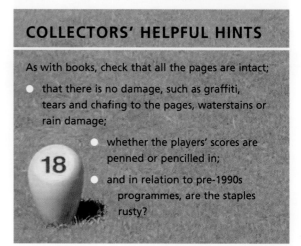

COLLECTORS' HELPFUL HINTS

As with books, check that all the pages are intact;

- that there is no damage, such as graffiti, tears and chafing to the pages, waterstains or rain damage;

- whether the players' scores are penned or pencilled in;

- and in relation to pre-1990s programmes, are the staples rusty?

Admission tickets add value to the relevant programme... so don't throw anything away.

modern programmes for three reasons: firstly, Max Faulkner won the Open, one of a small handful of British post-war winners, and it would be eighteen more years before another British player would achieve a similar success; secondly, it was the only time that the Championship has been played on a course not on the British mainland (it was in Northern Ireland); and thirdly, the weather wasn't good that week and consequently the majority of programmes were damaged by rain and the elements.

Further enhancements to the programme would be the relevant day pass/tickets to the event, and the daily order of play draw sheets; pre-1979 Open programmes contained detachable tear-out vouchers exchangeable for the daily draw sheets.

Programmes are marvellous mementos of the great championships, and their value can be enhanced by the status of the winner; for example as a winner, Jack

BUYER BEWARE

OUT OF BOUNDS

In other areas of programme collecting, such as football, there have been a number of illegal reprints or rare and important programmes. These are not easily recognized by the novice collector. Also, very good and virtually indiscernible repairs can be made to damaged pages, and this affects values considerably. Although these factors have not been witnessed in the arena of golf programme collecting, they could arise in the future when values increase.

Nicklaus or Tiger Woods would add serious value, whereas a one-off winner such as Ben Curtis in modern times wouldn't.

Harvie Ward won this silver
'Low Amateur' trophy at the 1957
Masters. He also finished fourth overall.

GOLF'S COLLECTABLE THEMES

Some collectors will restrict themselves to very specialized areas, for example only one of the four Majors such as the Open Championship, or just one great player such as Tiger Woods. Another notable single theme could be royalty, because over the centuries many of the royals have played the game. In this chapter, we will look at some of the many specialist collecting themes that transcend all aspects of the hobby, and will concentrate on two examples of a golfing event and three players from different generations.

The Masters

For many, the Masters is the harbinger of spring, the new golfing season, something to be looked forward to with great anticipation. Collecting Masters' memorabilia is very popular, especially in the United States, whether it is entrance badges for the public (almost as

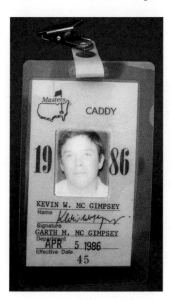

The author managed to play one shot at the Masters in 1986, an eight iron at the twefth.

hard to get after the event as during!), caddies' badges or contestants' badges.

In 1986 I was a caddie at the Masters – which was the Masters that the forty-six-year-old Jack Nicklaus won. I was carrying the bag of my brother Garth, who had been invited as the 1985 Amateur Champion. The whole experience was quite surreal. As soon as I had finished my caddie duties, I would leave my white

THE MASTERS

Between 1934 and 1938, the Masters, as it is known today, was promoted as The Augusta National Invitation Tournament. The Masters Tournament (not Championship) dates back to 1934.

Tom Morris: 1821–1908. Tom Morris (later referred to as 'Old Tom') was apprenticed at the age of eighteen as a feather ball maker to Allan Robertson. In due course he became one of the premier players of his day, a very good ball and club maker. Tom Morris was thirty-nine at the time of the inaugural Open Championship in 1860 and probably past his best, yet he managed to win it four times and was proud of his record of having played in every Open between 1860 and 1896. In 1864, he returned to St Andrews from an appointment at Prestwick, as the R & A's first professional and green keeper.

Bobby Jones: 1902–1971. Was he the greatest amateur golfer ever? Yes, he was! He won the Amateur in 1930; the Open in 1926, 1927 and 1930; the US Amateur in 1924, 1925, 1927, 1928 and 1930; and the US Open in 1923, 1926, 1929 and 1930. Some record.

The 1934 programme usually sells for more than £5,000.

overall and badge with the caddie master. I would then change into smart but casual wear, don my gold badge and walk into the clubhouse. This marvellous badge opened all doors – the only place I could not access was the Past Champions Locker Room. One lunchtime I remember being in the clubhouse and listening to David Graham, arguing or debating with fellow competitors that it was 'British Open' rather than 'The Open'. Maybe he had his own agenda, being an Australian and a winner of the US Open! Even then I was a keen golf historian and was starting to collect golfing memorabilia. But I did not ask for one autograph that week, even though there were always a number of players in the clubhouse, such as Seve Ballesteros, Arnold Palmer, Jack Nicklaus, Sandy Lyle *et al*. Of course it wouldn't have been appropriate if I had crossed the line of decorum, as it was the players' sanctum and refuge. So I controlled my collector urges, and didn't offend anyone or embarrass myself or my brother.

Each year the Augusta National Board of Governors continues to send printed black-on-white invitations, known as 'Masters Invitations', to the players. These invitations remain elusive, because the recipients cherish them so much and they seldom come on to the collectors' market. In fact ephemera from early Masters Tournaments are really difficult to find, and the 'flag-through-the-Georgia-badge' memorabilia must be one of the best known iconic symbols collected worldwide.

Undoubtedly, one of the most desirable pieces of Masters' memorabilia is the 1934 'First Annual Invitation Tournament, Augusta National Golf Club' forty-four-page programme. Measuring 11 x 8½in (28 x 21.5cm), it comprised several photograph portraits of the invited players, golf course illustrations, and even, ironically, some advertisements (ironic because in modern times The Masters doesn't 'do' advertising, and has remained a great golf event free of sponsors). The 1934 programme is rated as being exceedingly rare, and usually sells for more than £5,000. There was also a programme for the 1935 Masters, and this, too, is a sought-after item and sells for a similar price. In fact, some believe that the 1935 programme is even more elusive than the 1934 one.

In 1998, Augusta issued a replica of the 1934 programme. It is distinguished by the quality of the print and the paper, and has a collectable value in its own right of around £100 or so.

It was not until 1990 that the next Masters programme was published. These are glossy and filled with colour photographs and player profiles, and are undoubtedly collectables of the future. Also each year from 1978, the Augusta National issued Masters *Annuals* or *Yearbooks*. These are great founts of knowledge but are not very commercial, as yet.

THE ESOTERIC GREEN JACKET

Who would not want to own a Green Jacket, surely the most esoteric item of Augusta memorabilia, and show it off to their friends? Not so easy because these ultimate Masters' icons never leave Augusta? Not so! Gary Player brought his jacket back for the 1962 event as defending champion. But Arnold Palmer beat him into second place after an eighteen-hole play-off on the Monday, and after the award ceremony Player packed his jacket in his suitcase and flew back to South Africa. When the Masters chairman Mr Roberts learned that

Surely the ultimate prize for the collector of Masters memorabilia – the Green Jacket.

Player's jacket was not hanging in the champions' locker room, he rang Player and asked that it be returned. He was politely told that when he next came to Johannesburg, Player would meet him and return it. Mr Roberts 'backed down' and told Player he could keep it, but it was not to be worn in public. The next year Player was given a 'replacement' jacket, and that one remains at Augusta.

The first Green Jackets appeared in 1937, three years after the first tournament, and were worn by the members as a recognition aide for visitors. In 1949 Sam Snead became the first Masters champion to be presented with a Green Jacket to show that he was now an honorary member of Augusta National. Until 1966, the jackets were made by firms such as the Brooks Uniform Company, and then tailored locally in Augusta. Since 1967 the Hamilton Tailoring Company of Cincinnati, Ohio, has had the contract to supply the

green jacket to Augusta National. The gold-effect brass buttons are made by Waterbury Inc. of Connecticut. However, to complicate matters, members can order 'upmarket' bespoke jackets from Henry Poole, one of London's top Saville Row tailors. However, one significant difference between a member's jacket and a champion's jacket is that in recent times the buttons feature the word 'Masters'.

It is thought that over the years at least ten Green Jackets have 'escaped' Augusta. A member's jacket sold at auction in the early 2000s for $32,000, but the best one of all was the very jacket owned and worn by Robert T. Jones. This one came to auction in the late 1990s and sold for $95,000!

TICKETS AND BADGES

Until 1951, the Masters Champion received a wooden plaque inscribed 'Masters Tournament/Augusta

The winner at Augusta National receives a gold medal as well as a Green Jacket.

Great value for $25 in 1973: four days at the Masters!

National Golf Club'. Since then, the winner receives a round 10ct gold medal. The obverse in relief shows the Augusta clubhouse within a border, with a relief inscription in white 'Augusta National Golf Club'. The reverse has in relief the Augusta National Golf Club's emblem, and the inscription 'Masters Tournament'. It measures 1¾in (4.5cm). There are none known to have sold publicly at auction.

Ephemera and memorabilia such as tickets from the early Masters Tournaments are difficult to find. A good example of this would be the tie-on cardboard admission tickets issued for the 'Practice Rounds'. In 1935, the paying public were charged $1 plus 10 cents tax to get in on one of the practice days. During the 1970s the admission tickets went plastic, and the 1972 ones featured a facsimile signature of R. T. Jones. As these were usually discarded after the event, such items are rare and commercial. Some collectors will pay a big premium for a really low numbered badge, those under ten.

All competitors to the Masters get a numbered player's badge. They are allocated in the order that the players register. However, the defending champion is automatically given the No. 1 badge. Today these are usually made from a combination of metal and plastic, and their shape varies between square, rectangle and round. There is a story about Colin Montgomerie, who regards the number twenty-three (his birthday in June) as being his lucky number: if he arrived at Augusta and found that the officials had, for instance, only got down

to No. 20, he would hang back so that two players could register ahead of him!

Plastic entrance badges were introduced in 1961, and these, too, are popular items to collect, with collectors seeking special years such as Jack Nicklaus' last Masters win in 1986, or trying to complete runs of years, such as throughout the 1970s. A particularly nice Masters badge was the one issued in 2001. Measuring 4 x 2¾in (10 x 6cm), it nostalgically featured a photograph image of a young Bobby Jones. A run of post-war entrance badges would retail for £2,500 plus.

Other Masters items to collect would include Masters Golf Tournament press badges and season badges; or the books written about the event, including *The Masters Tournament*, an album compiled by Jones and Roberts and published in 1952, given to 'those who had actively contributed to the success of the Masters Tournament'. When offered for sale, it usually fetches over £1,000. Another book is a 1976 publication entitled *The Story of the Augusta National Golf Club*, written by Clifford Roberts. It was a very special limited edition, and the author signed each book.

PAINTINGS AND JEWELLERY

There have been many wonderful paintings done of the course, and American artist Linda Hartough is probably the best-known modern painter. Her originals of Augusta usually sell for in excess of £20,000.

Occasionally Augusta makes a memento for the players' wives and partners. For example in the early 1970s, they were given a lovely 14ct gold brooch in the shape of the Masters logo and trimmed with Masters green enamel. These seldom come on to the collectors' market.

And talking of mementos! A few years ago, a collector friend of mine was an expert at a golfing antiques Road Show being held at the Masters. A small gold charm decorated with an engraving of the Augusta national clubhouse was shown to the experts. It had belonged to Henry Picard (Masters Champion, 1938), and was engraved with his name. They quickly worked out what it was, and its significance in golf memorabilia circles. When Ben Hogan hosted the inaugural Champions' Dinner in 1952, he not only laid on a great Texan meal for his fellow winners, but he went one further by giving them a great memento. He had commissioned a small quantity of gold charms that were in the shape of the Masters' logo and opened up to reveal four panels. They were presented that evening by Hogan to his fellow members of the 'Masters Club' (not Augusta National), mainly all winners of the Masters. Hogan thought it appropriate to make Roberts and Jones (organizers of the Masters, but who were not Masters winners) honorary members of the new Masters Club.

Ryder Cup menu cards are very collectible.

My friend knew Gene Sarazen's daughter Maryann, and the next time he saw her, he asked her if she owned or remembered such a piece of jewellery. She recollected that her father had given it to her when she was a young girl, and it had been attached to her charm bracelet. She was at that time in the process of selling her father's Marco Island home and had been cleaning the house and throwing things out. She looked for the charm and eventually discovered it in a bin sack that was destined for the rubbish dump!

Each charm had a picture of the clubhouse on one panel; engraved on another panel was the name of the champion – in this case it was 'Gene Sarazen Member Masters Club, Augusta Georgia'; another panel was engraved 'Ben Hogan, Clifford Roberts and Robert Jones'; and the fourth panel depicted a picture of Ben Hogan and the initials of the recipient.

The Ryder Cup

One of the most popular 'new' collecting themes is everything to do with the Ryder Cup. There is a vast array of Ryder Cup memorabilia to collect, ranging from programmes, draw sheets, tickets, badges, ribbons, photographs, autographs, armbands, blazer crests, actual players' bags, ladies' brooches and pendants or items

RIGHT: Samuel Ryder's putter that sold at auction in 2008 for £18,000.

LEFT: Ben Crenshaw successfully based the design of his 1999 Ryder Cup menu on the artwork of the 1927 menu.

RIGHT: The 1933 and 1937 Ryder Cup matches were played at Southport and Ainsdale.

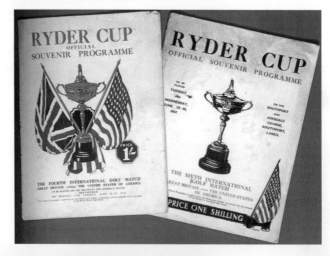

BELOW: Usually the American Ryder Cup programmes are of a much larger format than those of Great Britain and Ireland or Europe.

RIGHT: Peter Oosterhuis was a great Ryder Cup competitor…he is now a very good television commentator.

BELOW: These Ryder Cup money clips act as players' ID badges.

BELOW: Very rare and delicate, pre-war Ryder Cup bibs showing the Stars and Stripes, the Union Flag and the Tricolour of Ireland.

BELOW LEFT: As an alternative to the Ryder Cup, many collect the amateur equivalent: the Walker Cup.

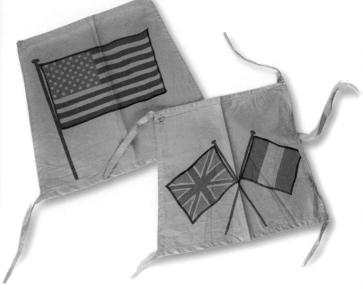

ABOVE: Ryder Cup necklaces and pendants as worn by the players' wives and girlfriends.

LEFT: The 1987 European Ryder Cup team wore this player's gilt badge – traditionally the American team give Ryder Cup necklaces and brooches to the wives and girl friends of the visitors.

COLLECTORS' HELPFUL HINTS

- Clothing not associated with players, such as ties and polo shirts, is in little demand.
- Who knows whether 2001 Ryder Cup memorabilia will rocket in value?
- Limited edition prints, especially when signed by the teams, remain strong.
- There is a wonderful display of Ryder Cup memorabilia at Valderrama in Spain.

associated with actual Ryder Cup players. And of course there is much over-lapping with other collectable themes.

It had been a tradition at the Amateur equivalent, the Walker Cup, to have either a welcoming reception or a farewell dinner, or both, for the participating teams and officials. This was considered appropriate for the Ryder Cup too, and so the American PGA laid on a complimentary banquet for its British visitors at the first Ryder Cup held in 1927. These were printed to record for posterity the usually very sumptuous courses as well as the date of the function, the venue, the toasts, and sometimes even the teams and the results of the matches. During the meal, players invariably would ask their fellow players to sign the menu as a souvenir of the

Max Faulkner played on five Ryder Cup teams.

match and the reception. Menus are, by their nature, disposable items of ephemera, and surviving ones are consequently rare. Only six Ryder Cups were played before World War II, and the menus are collectable and valuable. The 1999 Brookline menu card was designed to have a 1920/30s feel and appearance. Being somewhat of a golf memorabilia collector and traditionalist, Ben Crenshaw, who was the 1999 USA team captain, used the design of the 1927 menu as a basis for the 1999 menus. The menu that is hardest to find is for the 1933 Ryder Cup; in fact, was one even produced?

Team money clips, usually gold plated or in yellow or white metal, were originally introduced by the American Ryder Cup team in the post World War II period. These double up as players' ID badges to get access to the clubhouse, putting green, practice ground and first tee. White stones were used up until 1987 to denote the captain's clip; blue stones were always used for the team players' clip; silver/white metal was used from 1951 to 1963; and gold/yellow metal used from 1965 to 1977. In 1979 'GB & Ireland' was changed to 'European'. A rare modern set would be the ones produced for the cancelled 2001 event due to '9/11'. Each clip featured the red and blue enamel Ryder Cup motif, and each one was individually engraved with the team player.

The more valuable money clips are the ones named with a player, as this signifies they were 'official' as opposed to maybe being extra manufacturers' stock, or samples not used at the time by the relevant PGA.

SAM RYDER

Few amateurs who took up golf after their fiftieth birthday have left as many positive impressions upon the game as Samuel Ryder. Born in 1858, he was the son of a Manchester corn merchant and educated at Manchester University. After his studies, Ryder joined his father's business until he came up with the idea of selling penny seed packets to garden lovers. Unfortunately later he became ill, due to overwork. His doctor encouraged him to take up golf.

After initial golf lessons, Ryder went on to retain Abe Mitchell as his personal golf coach at an annual fee of £1,000. Mitchell was considered to be one of the finest British players not to have won an Open Championship. Ryder practised six days a week for a year at his home before applying for membership at the nearby Verulum Golf Club in St Albans in 1910. Samuel Ryder was now fifty-two, and was playing off a very respectable four handicap. Within a year he was elected Captain of Verulum.

Just before the General Strike of 1926 in Britain, a £3,000 appeal was launched to finance the GB & I Ryder Cup team's trip to America.

The British team departed Southampton on the *SS Aquitania* for America, and the first Ryder Cup took place in 1927 at the Worcester Country Club, Massachusetts, where the American team defeated the Great Britain team, 9$\frac{1}{2}$ to 2$\frac{1}{2}$. Samuel Ryder saw the first two Ryder Cup matches on home soil in 1929 and 1933.

Ryder died on 2 January 1936 aged seventy-seven. He was buried with his favourite mashie at the Trinity Congregational in St Albans.

Famous named players such as Palmer, Nicklaus and Woods will attract a premium price.

Walter Hagen, the American team captain for the first eleven years, takes credit for ensuring that his team at least was turned out smartly. Blazers were part of the uniform, and blazer badges featuring the Ryder Cup came into being in 1937. The 1939 Ryder Cup was cancelled due to the outbreak of hostilities. American Ryder

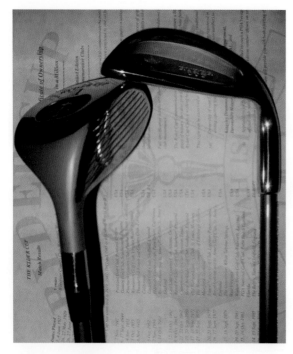

Maybe in time these two clubs, issued in 1991–1992, will appreciate in value!

Cup teams were selected in 1940–1944 to play against teams of professionals as fund-raisers for the American Red Cross and other charities.

Anything and everything associated with Sam Ryder himself is collected, ranging from his autograph, to photographs, to his very own putter that he used with great effect until he died.

In 1985, Tony Jacklin, the European Ryder Cup team captain, asked that every team member receive a gilt replica trophy, just as international footballers receive a 'cap'. These replicas are two-thirds the size of the original trophy. In September 2002, all surviving British, Irish and European Ryder Cup players were also presented with a replica trophy. This presentation was to have taken place in 2001, but was delayed because of the 9/11 tragedy. Asprey & Garrard made eighty-one trophies. In 2006, Bonhams' sold Max Faulkner's trophy for just over £4,000.

Ryder Cup memorabilia…possibly the worst buy? A company known as Kingsley Drummond marketed two 'official limited edition Ryder Cup commemorative' golf clubs between 1991 and 1992. The official 'blurb' stat-ed that the two clubs, a driver and a sand wedge, were struck to commemorate the match at Kiawah Island (known infamously as 'the war on the shore' Ryder Cup). Production was restricted to one set for every one million head of world population. I suppose when you take into account the populations of China and India, there were plenty of sets cast! The marketing blurb ran as follows: 'The Ryder Cup Commemorative Sand Wedge and Driver not only capture a little piece of history, they also give their owner an automatic right to purchase further Ryder Cup Clubs if wishing to make up a full or part set.'

As soon as you see 'limited edition' you should hear alarm bells ringing. Personally I would rather invest in an item that naturally wastes away, rather than having some marketing guru telling me what is limited and an investment. I would assume that too many were made; the reason for their being was spurious, and these clubs would not have been played with, hence they are all most likely in mint unused condition and still with original packaging and certificates.

Collecting a Famous Player

Some collectors have made it their hobby or life's work to concentrate solely on one player. We look at Tom Morris, but there are many others to be collected: Allan Robertson and Robert Forgan from the nineteenth century; Gene Sarazen and Walter Hagen for the 1930s and 1940s; Byron Nelson and Sam Snead in the 1940s and 1950s; Arnold Palmer, Jack Nicklaus and Gary Player in the 1960s and 1970s. The array and spectrum of memorabilia associated with such famous players is not confined to clubs; what about books, photographs, autographs, medals, trophies?

TOM MORRIS

His stamped long nose clubs are still regarded as being very desirable, and the collector should expect to pay a price from anywhere between £1,000 and £4,000 depending on how early the club was made. For golf ball collectors, a signed Tom Morris feathery ball is a must, but one of his few surviving hand-hammered gutty balls would be an ultimate possession. Although such surviving relics tend to be in golf club displays such

RIGHT: A rare Tom Morris feather golf ball from the 1850s. The marked area above the number '30' is where the final stitch to the twine has been made and concealed.

LEFT: Craig Campbell's portrait of Old Tom Morris commissioned in 2008.
RIGHT: Craig Campbell's oil of Tom Morris at St Andrews painted in 2008.

as at Muirfield, it is exciting when green keepers unearth valuable golf balls in some long-abandoned sand dune. In 2007 a Tom Morris gutty ball that had been found on the New Luffness links came to auction. The signature wasn't clear, but because it was Tom Morris it fetched nearly £1,000.

Of course golfing memorabilia does not have to be old to be collectable. In the late 1990s the well respected American sculptor M. Roche produced a very detailed limited edition metal study of Old Tom standing on the Swilken Bridge. Many think that this piece will be a great golf collectable in the future.

Golf books that mention Tom Morris are common, but the book that was entirely devoted to his life's story is a 'must have'. Written by Tulloch in 1908, it traced Tom's life and details, the matches he played, and the

events he won or lost. As with all old books, condition is a paramount factor in value, so expect to pay at least £500 for a good above-average copy of *The Life of Tom Morris, with Glimpses of St. Andrews and its Golfing Celebrities*. Old Tom, being golf's first super star, signed various studio portraits and postcards featuring his image, and there was a George Reid limited edition photogravure, pencil-signed by Tom in the white margin below the image. His autographs are still considered hard to find and are the cornerstone of a good collection.

Tom Senior and Young Tom.

A great collection of 'The Colossus of Golf' artefacts.

RIGHT: A clear Tom Morris signature is worth at least £500 today.

ABOVE AND RIGHT: Michael Roche's Old Tom Morris, Keeper of the Greens'.

COLLECTORS' HELPFUL HINTS

With 2008 marking the centenary of Tom Morris's death, it was apt that a new definitive book was published.

How would you put a value on a handful of life insurance policies in the name of Tom Morris? They were taken out as securities for the mortgage or bank loan when he was setting up his shop in St Andrews. They belong to Tom Morris' descendants. Answers please to the author on a Tom Morris postcard.

ROBERT T. JONES

Although Francis Ouimet was the first great American amateur golfer, it is Robert T. Jones Junior who is acknowledged as being the best amateur ever. As with other aspects of the hobby, there are many crossovers in the collecting fields to include the Masters, competitors' badges, Open programmes, autographs and golf clubs.

Jones was eventually commercially linked to Spalding, and the Robert Jones signatured, hickory-shafted irons released in 1930 were only available for a year before being replaced with metal-shafted clubs. A set of these earlier irons would sell at auction for five times that of the metal ones. They remain very popular with today's hickory competition players. Imagine not only playing with the same clubs as designed by the great Bobby Jones, but how about playing with one he played with?

One of the rarest Robert Tyre Jones clubs known to exist is a No.6 iron that was actually made for and owned by him. It was made by Scottish club maker Tom Stewart, and it has his dot denoting that Stewart personally made the club; the V mark signified that Tom Stewart's head foreman had supervised the making of the club. Unlike all standard Jones signature irons that had his name lying horizontally on the back of the club, this No.6 iron has his signature in a vertical position. This iron was sold in 2007 for a sum in excess of £15,000.

The Robert Jones signature is still a great collectable. Basically there were four styles of Jones' signature over the years that were dependent on his age, health and who he was 'signing' for. Jones signed as 'Bob' all his life to people he knew.

So there are 'vintage' Bob Jones autographs, and vintage Robt T. Jones, Jr. autographs; and every once in a while he would write the entire 'Robert', but not often. At the end of his life when he was so severely crippled by bad health that he had to use a large ball device to rest his hand whilst penning his signature. These, usually very shaky autographs are not as valuable as the clear, strong ones from the 1930s.

LEFT: A rare Bobby Jones-signed Spalding ball that sold at auction in 2005 for £5,500.
BELOW: A clean Bobby Jones autograph is always sought after – value £600.

Note how the Robert T. Jones signature and the No.6 are at right angles to the normal position, strongly suggesting that this was one of his personal irons.

ABOVE: Tiger Woods won the 2006 USPGA at Medinah. LEFT: Tiger Woods signing at Royal LIverpool in 2006. ABOVE RIGHT: This signed print shows how Tiger Wood's signature has changed since the year 2000.

A 10ct gold PGA of America signet ring with cast lettering, 'T. Woods' and 'Member' sold at auction for £5,000.

There are several original paintings of Jones hanging in the golf clubs that are associated with him, and their copies adorn hundreds of golf clubs around the world. Collectors are still fascinated with Bobby Jones and his Grand Slam feat, and consequently 1930 golf badges and programmes for events that Jones played in are keenly sought after. Collectors tend to imagine that the contestant who wore this badge may have been Jones himself; or that if he wasn't, then as a contestant in the Amateur he may have played against Jones (and lost) or maybe he stood beside Jones whilst on the practice ground. For collectors it is all to do with association, and for many there isn't a more significant golfer from the past to be associated with.

There were many books written on Bobby Jones, biographies and autobiographies and these make for a great book collection, especially the ones signed by Jones.

TIGER WOODS

Signed Tiger Woods items are very much in demand today. The biggest problem is the inordinately huge number of fake Tiger Woods that are always for sale on

Craig Campbell's painting of Tiger Woods in 2007 is superb.

TIGER WOODS

Eldrick Tiger Woods was born on 30 December 1975 in Cypress, California. An outstanding amateur golfer who won three consecutive US Amateur Championships (1994–1996), he played in six major championships and made the cut in four of them. In the 1996 Open at Royal Lytham, he equalled the eighteen-hole amateur record with a sixty-six.

He turned professional in August 1996, joined the US Tour full time in 1997, and won his first Major, the Masters, in April of that year. Two million people under the age of eighteen tried golf for the first time in America in the week following Wood's win. Television viewing figures showed that more than twice as many people followed his progress compared with the epic shoot-out the previous year involving Nick Faldo and Greg Norman.

By August 2005 he had won a further three Masters, two US Opens, two Opens and two USPGA Championships. His third Open victory at Royal Liverpool in 2006 made it eleven Major titles. Undoubtedly the dominant figure of modern-day golf, Woods became the first player to hold all four Majors simultaneously when he won the Open, the US Open and the USPGA in 2000, followed by the Masters in 2001. As of July 2008 his record in the Majors is:

- The Masters: He has four titles and needs two to join Jack Nicklaus on six.
- The US Open: With three wins he needs one more to join Willie Anderson, Bobby Jones, Ben Hogan and Jack Nicklaus on four.
- The Open: Tiger could break the longest-standing record, the six Opens won by Harry Vardon. He has three Claret Jugs.
- The USPGA: Tiger has won four times and needs one more to match the five of Walter Hagen and Jack Nicklaus.
- Total: fourteen Majors.

the various Internet sites. Obviously they cannot all be fakes, but the buyer really does have to beware. His management team maintains a close watch on what he is asked to sign. Tiger will now not autograph a golf ball because it is too easy to reproduce a signature that for obvious reasons is not as his normal signature looks.

On occasions, Tiger has signed limited edition prints. For example in 1998, Craig Campbell had a special edition of only 125 prints of an original oil that showed Tiger in four different poses. Tiger signed the original painting and signed the prints, as did Craig Campbell. When these come to auction they fetch over £800.

One of the strangest and most personal Tiger Woods items to be sold recently was a 1997 PGA signet ring stamped with his name. He gave it to his caddie, who in turn sold it on with written guarantees of authenticity. It sold for over £5,000 in 2006.

INDEX